WHERE WE'RE BORN

BY LUCY THURBER

DRAMATISTS
PLAY SERVICE
INC.

SPECIAL NOTE

Anyone receiving permission to produce WHERE WE'RE BORN is required to give credit to the Author as sole and exclusive Author of the Play on the title page of all programs distributed in connection with performances of the Play and in all instances in which the title of the Play appears for purposes of advertising, publicizing or otherwise exploiting the Play and/or a production thereof. The name of the Author must appear on a separate line, in which no other name appears, immediately beneath the title and in size of type equal to 50% of the size of the largest, most prominent letter used for the title of the Play. No person, firm or entity may receive credit larger or more prominent than that accorded the Author. The following acknowledgment must appear on the title page in all programs distributed in connection with performances of the Play:

World Premiere produced by Rattlestick Playwrights Theater.

SPECIAL NOTE ON SONGS AND RECORDINGS

For performances of copyrighted songs, arrangements or recordings mentioned in this Play, the permission of the copyright owner(s) must be obtained. Other songs, arrangements or recordings may be substituted provided permission from the copyright owner(s) of such songs, arrangements or recordings is obtained; or songs, arrangements or recordings in the public domain may be substituted.

WHERE WE'RE BORN was produced by Rattlestick Playwrights Theater in New York City, opening on November 17, 2003. It was directed by Will Frears; the set design was by Takeshi Kata; the costume design was by Jenny Mannis; the lighting design was by Matthew Richards; and the sound design was by Fitz Patton. The cast was as follows:

LILLY .... Marin Ireland
TONY .... Thomas Sadoski
FRANKY .... Sara Surrey
VIN .... Jason Pugatch
DREW .... Patch Darragh

CHARACTERS

LILLY MARINO
TONY MARINO
FRANKY LaRUE
VIN WRIGHT
DREW AVERY

PLACE

A hill town in western Massachusetts.

TIME

The present.

WHERE WE'RE BORN

ACT ONE

The time is the present, it is fall. It is late afternoon. A hill town in western Massachusetts. A house in the center of town that has been turned into apartments. There is a front porch, a door that leads into a kitchen/living room. There is a door upstage right that leads to a slightly elevated bedroom. Vin and Drew are climbing the steps of the front porch. Vin is carrying two six-packs of beer. He knocks on the front door. There is no answer.

VIN. Not home.
DREW. *(Pushing by Vin to knock on the door.)* Tony? Franky? You home?
VIN. What did I just tell you, shithead?
DREW. Maybe they didn't hear you. It's possible.
VIN. Here, *(He hands Drew a beer.)* Have a beer. *(They sit down, both opening beers. The sound of a car driving by. Vin and Drew turn their heads in unison from left to right.)* There goes Jim Price.
DREW. Yup.
VIN. You hear about him?
DREW. I heard he's screwing Don's wife.
VIN. Not anymore, Don caught 'um.
DREW. No?
VIN. That's what I heard.
DREW. I wouldn't fuck with Don. The Bryant boys love their guns.
VIN. Well, Don caught old Jimmy with his pants down.
DREW. No shit?
VIN. Yup. Don came home early, right, calling for his beer —
DREW. And found to his horror —
VIN. Yup, Jimmy went running for his truck with his pants around

his knees, and Don caught him half-way down the driveway and they start fist-fighting. Jimmy doesn't even have time to pull up his pants.
DREW. That would make me a little insecure.
VIN. Yup, Jimmy's hanging and swinging free in the wind. So about this time, Holly Parker drives by and a'course she slows down so she can get a better look. You know Holly's always been sweet on Jimmy and now she has a front-row seat to Jimmy's manhood. And while she's looking, Laurie comes out wrapped up only in a sheet. And Laurie starts begging Don to come in and have a beer.
DREW. Laurie's one dumb bitch.
VIN. Yup. And Holly a'course drives straight over to Jimmy's house to tell Sarah.
DREW. Holly's always causing trouble.
VIN. Yup.
DREW. Sarah's a bit touched too. Remember that Fourth of July party? She smashed Jimmy's windshield in with an ax.
VIN. Yeah I remember. So what do you think she did?
DREW. Um, I'd say gun.
VIN. That's right and goes running over to Don's house.
DREW. Shit.
VIN. Yup, but guess who's showed up in the meantime?
DREW. No?
VIN. You guessed it. Louie's there with his sirens going and he's pointing his gun at everyone telling them to freeze. Jimmy and Don are still trading punches and Laurie's screaming. It's one big mess. That's when Sarah comes charging in and starts firing her .22 into the air so everyone starts running for cover. And Jimmy's like, "Baby, put the gun down, honey, baby please ... " And then she points the gun straight at him and says, "I've had it with you! I'm telling my grandmother what you've been doing!" Then she gave him the sign. *(Vin makes the sign of the devil, passing his hand in a slow arc from right to left.)*
DREW. *(Shivering.)* Jesus Christ, what'd you do that for? *(He knocks on wood.)*
VIN. Just livin' on the edge. Sarah has got one spooky family, though.
DREW. Yeah, I stay out of their way.
VIN. Yup.
DREW. I bet that sent everyone home quick.
VIN. Yup. I saw Laurie later though, in the package store.

DREW. How'd she look?
VIN. Pretty bad.
DREW. Damn. Don's one mean drunk. I don't hang out with him no more.
VIN. Nope. That shit's bullshit. *(Lights up on Tony and Lilly in the bedroom of the apartment. Tony stands looking at himself in the mirror in the bedroom. Lilly sits on the bed watching him, a duffel bag beside her. He takes off his T-shirt and throws it on the floor.)*
TONY. *(Smelling his armpit.)* Jesus, I stink. *(He crosses to Lilly and pushes her face into his armpit.)* Don't I stink, Lill?
LILLY. *(Pushing herself away from him.)* Yes, Tony, you do. *(Tony crosses to the closet, opens it and starts searching through clothes on the floor.)*
TONY. You can just keep your stuff in here. Franky won't mind. *(He crosses to the bed, picks up her duffel bag and throws it on the closet floor. He then continues to look through the clothes. He finds a shirt and puts it on.)*
LILLY. Your T-shirt's covered in shit Tony. *(Tony looks down at himself.)*
TONY. Damn. I thought these was the clothes she washed.
LILLY. Guess not. *(Tony takes off his shirt and throws it on the ground. He looks through clothes again. He pulls out another T-shirt and flannel. He puts the T-shirt on. He looks at himself in the mirror again.)*
TONY. Who's beautiful?
LILLY. You are.
TONY. Damn right. *(He makes a muscle in the mirror and punches it. Lilly laughs. He winks at her. He turns to her, still making a muscle.)* Well?
LILLY. Strongest man in the world.
TONY. And don't you ever forget it. *(Tony turns back to the mirror and combs his hair. Turning back to her:)* I look OK?
LILLY. Yeah.
TONY. Good. *(There is a pause. He lights a cigarette. Looks at her.)*
LILLY. What?
TONY. I think you know.
LILLY. No, I don't. Can I have one of those? *(Tony gives her a cigarette and lights it for her.)*
TONY. Don't make me do this. Don't play stupid with me.
LILLY. You're upset about something.
TONY. You know I am.
LILLY. And you want me to guess what it is?

TONY. You know what it is. *(Pause, he looks at her.)*
LILLY. Yeah, OK. I do. But what did you want me to do about it?
TONY. You said you'd be home for your mother's birthday.
LILLY. I'm here now —
TONY. Your mother was very upset and who could blame her.
LILLY. Fuck my mother.
TONY. Watch your fucken mouth, Lilly.
LILLY. Sorry … look, I had an opportunity to make some money. I took it. I need it. You don't understand how expensive the books are and —
TONY. I understand that but —
LILLY. You couldn't possibly —
TONY. Watch it! What's wrong with you? You forget who you're talking to?
LILLY. No.
TONY. It seems like you did.
LILLY. No.
TONY. You haven't been home once since you got there. Don't tell me that one of those little rich friends of yours couldn't have driven you home for a visit, like that boyfriend of yours with the car —
LILLY. Tony, come on, he's not my boyfriend —
TONY. Don't act like I wouldn't have come and gotten you in a second if you'd asked —
LILLY. I know but you don't understand how busy it is —
TONY. I don't know who you're hanging out with over there, if I didn't know better —
LILLY. What the fuck are you talking about — ?
TONY. I understand you got to adjust and all that shit but —
LILLY. I don't have a minute to breathe. It's hard, the work is hard and —
TONY. I know you can handle it —
LILLY. That's not what I'm saying —
TONY. You're too hard on yourself —
LILLY. Tony —
TONY. Hell, I would have given you some money —
LILLY. Tony, you don't understand, one book is like seventy-five dollars —
TONY. Shit …
LILLY. I'm trying to —
TONY. Well, I got your mom a present for you —

LILLY. Thanks, I —
TONY. Hell I did it for myself, I was tired of hearing her yapping —
LILLY. I'm sorry —
TONY. It doesn't matter to me. You know that. *(He looks at her. A small pause.)*
LILLY. I know that, Tony. It's not that it's —
TONY. I guess you're working hard over there, huh? *(He doesn't give her a chance to answer.)* Come here, kid. *(Tony hugs her.)*
LILLY. I just …
TONY. Don't get much of a break?
LILLY. No, I guess …
TONY. I'm gonna give you the best vacation you ever had. *(Lilly leans against Tony. She pats his stomach.)* Come on. *(He crosses to the closet, ruffles around and pulls out two baseball gloves.)*
LILLY. Now?
TONY. No time better. *(Tony and Lilly cross to the porch. Tony carries the gloves and ball.)*
DREW. *(To Vin.)* I told you he was home.
VIN. *(To Drew.)* Shut up, jackass.
TONY. *(To Vin and Drew.)* Look who's here.
VIN. *(To Lilly.)* What are you doing here? I thought you were in Northampton.
DREW. Lilly Marino, how the hell are you?
TONY. She's on her October vacation. I went to pick her up.
DREW. She wasn't here for her mom's birthday bash? Were you? Was I that drunk, Vin?
VIN. You're always that drunk, man.
TONY. *(He gives Lilly a glove.)* Let's play some catch. I wouldn't want to think the last two months ruined your arm. There's still some light left. Let's not waste it. *(He crosses down center to the bare stage and Lilly follows him. They begin to toss the ball back and forth.)* Would you look at the arm on that girl.
VIN. Yeah, she can throw.
DREW. That's right. Your cousin can throw. You glad to be home, Lilly?
LILLY. Very.
VIN. So you liking it? College?
LILLY. It's great.
DREW. I hear there's a lot of partying in college.
VIN. That's right.

DREW. Remember, what's-his-name, that kid from up on the hill?
TONY. *(To Lilly.)* High pop.
VIN. Charlie Nash.
DREW. That's right. Charlie Nash. He went to college, didn't he?
VIN. Not for long. Too much partying, they kicked his ass out the door. UMass?
TONY. *(To Lilly.)* Grounder.
DREW. He had some stories though, remember?
VIN. Yeah.
DREW. He said they had chem majors making acid, right on campus.
VIN. That's right.
TONY. Not at Amherst, right Lilly? Think quick.
DREW. Did we drive over there one night to party with Charlie?
VIN. I don't know. Hey Tony?
TONY. What?
VIN. Did we ever party with Charlie Nash at his college?
TONY. No.
VIN. I think we did.
TONY. We didn't.
VIN. Yeah, I think we did. Didn't we, Drew?
DREW. I don't know. I don't remember.
TONY. *(Catches the ball and holds it. To Vin and Drew:)* You know what her mother told me?
DREW. Nope.
VIN. Nope.
LILLY. What? She has another new boyfriend?
TONY. Don't be cute.
LILLY. Sorry. What did she tell you?
TONY. You're on the honor roll.
LILLY. Yeah …
TONY. Did you hear that, boys? She's on the honor roll.
VIN. Not surprised.
DREW. Nope. Not surprised.
VIN. All she ever did was read.
DREW. She always read a lot. Those weird books too.
VIN. Sure did. Too much reading will ruin your mind.
TONY. Don't be stupid, Vin. It's 'cause she reads so much she's gonna be rich. First Marino in the whole history of Marinos to go to college. Fuck, those people are paying her to think.
VIN. Yeah, like I think I'll drink a beer. Lilly, you want one?

LILLY. Yes please. *(Vin hands Lilly a beer.)* Thank you. *(She opens it. She takes a sip. Franky enters. She is wearing a waitress uniform and is carrying a six-pack of beer and a bottle of 151 rum.)*

DREW. Tony?

TONY. Yeah.

FRANKY. Hey. *(Vin nods in acknowledgment and in greeting.)*

DREW. Hey Franky, you're looking good as always.

FRANKY. Why thank you. How long you boys been here?

DREW. Not too long.

FRANKY. Uh-huh.

DREW. Not long, ain't that right, Vin?

VIN. Nope, not too long.

FRANKY. Naw, you guys are never here too long. Sometimes I have to wonder if you even have homes to go to. *(She puts down the six-pack at Vin's feet.)* Here, you're gonna drink it anyway. Hi, Lilly.

LILLY. Hi, Franky.

FRANKY. It's nice to have you home.

LILLY. Thanks.

FRANKY. You get here alright?

LILLY. Yeah.

FRANKY. Tony didn't keep you waiting, did he?

LILLY. No, right on time.

FRANKY. Well, that's a surprise. He keeps me waiting all the time. Don't you, Tony.

VIN. Here comes trouble.

DREW. Yup, trouble's a'coming.

FRANKY. *(To Vin and Drew.)* You two keep your mouths shut. Tony, I want to speak to you inside right now.

TONY. I'll tell you what, Franky, why don't you try not being so rude and say a proper hello to Lilly. Why don't you try that, before you start ordering me around.

LILLY. Tony, come on, she already did.

TONY. I don't call that a proper hello —

FRANKY. You want proper? Try this on for size, you ain't getting your hands on anything proper unless you get your ass inside right now and talk to me. Move. *(She exits into the bedroom.)*

LILLY. Tony, it's OK. Just go talk to her —

TONY. Lilly, it's not OK —

LILLY. Tony, just talk to Franky.

TONY. Shit …

VIN. Keep the faith, man.

DREW. Yeah, be strong and when you're done we can drink the bottle of 151 she brought you. Can't say she doesn't love you, man.

VIN. Loves you loads.

TONY. Both of you shut the fuck up. *(He crosses to the bedroom. Lights fade on the porch and up on Tony and Franky as he enters the bedroom.)*

FRANKY. It's a small town, Tony.

TONY. Yeah? No shit.

FRANKY. You like embarrassing me?

TONY. What the fuck are you talking about now?

FRANKY. Tony, you know.

TONY. Don't start with me. Why do you always gotta act so crazy, huh?

FRANKY. I ain't acting crazy!

TONY. Sure you are, bothering me the way you do. That's crazy.

FRANKY. Tony, I'm pissed. You see me being pissed? All I do is try to make something for us and all you do is shit on it.

TONY. What are you yapping about now? You need to just shut up!

FRANKY. Don't tell me to shut up!

TONY. Shut up! *(Vin, Drew and Lilly enter into the house and sit in the living room.)*

VIN. *(From the living room. Calling to them:)* Why don't you both shut up!

TONY. *(Opening the bedroom door.)* Shut the fuck up! *(Slamming the bedroom door.)* Jesus, in my own fucken house. *(Pause.)*

FRANKY. You go out in public with her, Tony?

TONY. What?

FRANKY. Where everyone can see?

TONY. What are you talking about now?!

FRANKY. Everybody's laughing at me, Tony. I go out and the whole town starts laughing at me.

TONY. *(Going to her.)* Nobody's laughing at you, baby.

FRANKY. Tony, they're laughing at me

TONY. *(Kissing her.)* Nobody's laughing.

FRANKY. I just saw that bitch of yours in the package store. You don't think her and all her little friends started laughing at me?

TONY. Franky —

FRANKY. You don't think I felt like the biggest shit that ever lived standing there holding a bottle of 151 rum? And you know that slut felt she had the right to walk up to me and comment on how much you love to drink it?

TONY. I'm …

FRANKY. Now I know you don't want me to embarrass you in front of Lilly. I don't know why you can't have the same respect for me and not —

TONY. There ain't a person in this town that don't know you're with me. *(He crosses to her and kisses her.)* There ain't a person who doesn't know how much I love you. *(He kisses her again, she pulls away and starts towards the door.)* Where are you going now?

FRANKY. I'm going to change. We've got company, Tony. And I'm nothing if not a good host. *(Light switch. Drew is sitting on the couch. Vin is standing stage right of the couch, by the stereo, looking through tapes. Lilly is watching them.)*

DREW. How 'bout Skynyrd?

VIN. Nope.

DREW. *Led Zeppelin II*?

VIN. No.

DREW. What you putting in then?

VIN. You'll see. *(Vin finds the tape he wants and puts it in. He hits rewind.)*

DREW. I had another crazy dream last night.

VIN. Yeah? You gotta stop having those dreams, man.

DREW. Yeah, yeah I know. *(The tape finishes rewinding. Vin presses play. Music that sounds like Jimi Hendrix plays.* Vin and Drew sing along with the beginning of the tape. The tape plays under the rest of the scene. Franky and Tony come into the living room from the bedroom.)*

VIN. You two done?

TONY. Yeah, we're done. Right, baby? *(Franky crosses and goes out onto the porch.)*

VIN. Not quite done, I guess.

TONY. Shit. Light one up, boys. What you say, Lilly? Time to get high? *(Vin takes out pot and starts to roll a joint. Drew crosses out to the porch. Throughout Drew and Franky's scene, Vin finishes rolling the joint and Tony, Lilly and Vin smoke. Lights dim on them, up on Drew and Franky.)*

DREW. Did you know some of those stars aren't really there?

* See Special Note on Songs and Recordings on copyright page.

FRANKY. Yeah right.
DREW. It's 'cause light takes so long to travel. Some of that light is thousands of years old. Think about that for a minute. Light that's older than we are. Light that thinks we're nothing. Like trees.
FRANKY. Trees?
DREW. Some trees are pretty old. Like that one over there. I bet some Indian climbed that tree. Some pilgrim hanged another pilgrim for stealing or something from that tree. Now, here we are just looking at it. That tree could tell us some excellent stories.
FRANKY. Yeah? Like what?
DREW. Shhh, listen. *(Pause.)* You hear it?
FRANKY. No.
DREW. It could almost be the wind blowing. It's singing, wind and rain, deep dark earth. The roots pushing down past rocks and worms.
FRANKY. You're poetic, Drew. My cousin's like you. She's always seeing things. Says she sees spirits and shit, I don't know. But she always knows just who it is when the phone rings. What else you see up there, huh?
DREW. Sparkles and the colors. It's like the air is water with fireflies in it.
FRANKY. You've been smoking out all day, haven't you, Drew? But that's cool. I seen shit like that when I'm tripping. *(She slaps Drew on the back playfully.)* Hey, your born-again daddy know you talk like this? *(Silence. Drew will not look at her.)* You're a good kid, Drew. I've always thought so.
DREW. Shit.
FRANKY. Don't get shy on me now.
DREW. I ain't.
FRANKY. Yeah you are.
DREW. Why'd ya think I'm shy?
FRANKY. You're shy around girls. You ought to get yourself someone.
DREW. What makes you say that?
FRANKY. I never see you with anyone.
DREW. Just 'cause you don't see it, doesn't mean it's not there. Besides, they'd have to be pretty special for me to bring them around here, wouldn't they? *(Tony sticks out the front door.)*
TONY. Hey Frank.
FRANKY. Yeah.
TONY. You gotta come in and tell Vin what you told me about Kristy Johnson.

FRANKY. What about her? *(Tony comes all the way out onto the porch, as he does lights come up full on the living room.)*
TONY. Tell Vin what Tammy Graves told you about what she did with her insurance money. *(Vin calls from the living room.)*
VIN. It's a bunch of bullshit!
TONY. *(Calling back to him.)* No it's not, and if you weren't such a shithead, you'd know it. *(To Franky.)* Please baby, come back in and tell him. Haven't you been out here long enough?
FRANKY. I don't know.
TONY. Sure you do. *(He kisses her. Drew stands awkwardly for a moment watching them kiss and then crosses from the porch into the living room.)*
VIN. *(To Drew.)* Do you believe this shit he's saying? *(Tony and Franky cross to the living room, lights down on the porch.)*
FRANKY. It's not shit. It's the truth.
VIN. Fuck you.
FRANKY. Trust me. They're not real.
DREW. Bullshit.
FRANKY. Nu-uh, after the accident, she got a shitload of insurance money. They ain't real.
VIN. They felt real to me.
DREW. Vin would know.
VIN. That's right. And they're as real as they come.
FRANKY. You wouldn't know real from a hole in your head. The things are filled with some kid of jellyroll.
DREW. What flavor? She looks peach to me. Vin?
VIN. Melon. I'd say she definitely tastes like melon. She's about the size of a melon, that's for sure.
DREW. Vin likes melon.
VIN. Damn right! Who doesn't?
DREW. I've been thinking.
VIN and TONY. Oh shit.
DREW. No, I've been thinking about fucken college girls, Lilly. Me and Vin should come visit you and cause a little ruckus. Get us some college girls. Right, Vin?
VIN. Damn right.
DREW. Though me and Vin been doing alright, since you left. Tony tell you about all the pussy we been getting?
TONY. I told her about how you never get laid.
VIN. I get laid.

TONY. Yeah, you get laid. *(To Drew.)* But you haven't seen pussy in years. I heard you like to visit the sheep.
DREW. Yeah, right. You got Franky and you still visit sheep.
VIN. A man can get a sheep pregnant.
TONY. Bullshit.
VIN. It's true. They can't carry 'em long, but they can get pregnant.
DREW. That's bullshit if I ever heard it.
VIN. My cousin told me! He even found some of the miscarried babies.
TONY. Fuck you, he did.
VIN. No fuck you, he told me!
DREW. Hey Tony, you think you got some half-formed sheep sons?
TONY. Fuck you too! I never fuck sheep, you're the one who fucks sheep.
DREW. Why you getting so mad then?
TONY. 'Cause you're both full of it, that's why.
LILLY. Now Tony, that's no way to talk to your two best friends.
TONY. These motherfuckers are not my best friends.
LILLY. That's not what you told me.
DREW. Hey man, you told her that. Hey Tony, I know you don't fuck sheep.
VIN. That's sweet, man. You told her that. That's sweet. *(Tony goes to get a beer.)*
TONY. Shit, we're out of beer.
VIN. Packy run.
DREW. *(To Tony.)* Packy run, you coming?
TONY. Yeah. I'm the only one with a car, remember? *(To Franky.)* You want something special? Peppermint schnapps?
FRANKY. I'm OK, thanks.
TONY. Give me a kiss. *(Franky does. Tony, Vin and Drew cross to the porch, the women follow. The men exit, the women watch them go from the porch. A moment of silence.)*
FRANKY. Finally a little quiet.
LILLY. Yeah.
FRANKY. Sometimes I can't hear myself think.
LILLY. I know what you mean.
FRANKY. I know you do. I've missed you.
LILLY. Yeah. Why?
FRANKY. It's nice to have a little female company around the house. So … let's take a look at you.

LILLY. Do we have to?
FRANKY. You know we do.
LILLY. Yeah, I know …
FRANKY. *(Looking at her.)* Turn around. *(Lilly does.)* Very nice. You're looking good.
LILLY. You're a big fat liar.
FRANKY. You know I never lie.
LILLY. I know that's what you tell me.
FRANKY. Don't be cute. You look beautiful. I like those pants. They're a little different but they look good on you. Where did you get them?
LILLY. A second-hand store in Northampton.
FRANKY. A second-hand store?
LILLY. It's all the rage at school.
FRANKY. OK, if you say so.
LILLY. I do. And you're looking good, as always.
FRANKY. You sweet-talker.
LILLY. Just stating facts.
FRANKY. Well, thank you. I haven't been feeling too pretty these days.
LILLY. Why not?
FRANKY. I don't know, just tired, I guess. So anyway, enough about that. I want to know all about everything. Tony says you're doing really well, the honor roll, right?
LILLY. This quarter anyway.
FRANKY. And next, I'm sure.
LILLY. I hope so. It's hard to keep up.
FRANKY. Why?
LILLY. I mean the scholarship covers my tuition and I'm on the work-study program. But that barely covers my books, let alone anything else. I've been thinking of getting a job in town but honestly, I've never had so much reading in my life and the papers and the tests. And it's making me —
FRANKY. Terrified.
LILLY. Yeah.
FRANKY. What about all your friends? Tony says you have lots of friends.
LILLY. I guess. I feel like … I tell them stories, so they'll like me. I tell them about my mom and I tell 'um about getting beat up in school 'cause I read too much. And the more stories I tell them, the

more I kinda hate them all.
FRANKY. Ouch.
LILLY. Yeah.
FRANKY. It'll be OK.
LILLY. You think?
FRANKY. It has to be OK, doesn't it? So it just will. I mean, that's life, right? If that's the only way you can see something going … if you can only go in one … I mean, you know? *(Pause.)*
LILLY. What's wrong, Franky?
FRANKY. What do you mean?
LILLY. I mean … I don't know … why don't you feel pretty lately? *(Franky laughs.)* No … I mean you should, you should feel pretty all the time because you are pretty … you know, all the time.
FRANKY. So they tell me.
LILLY. And they're right. I mean hell … I always thought you were the prettiest girl in the world. I don't mean used to, I mean, I still —
FRANKY. Stop it Lilly —
LILLY. Why? I just wanted —
FRANKY. I know I'm pretty.
LILLY. Oh.
FRANKY. I've spent my whole life pretty. I know what that means. It's not that. It's just, you know how it is around here. I'm just always waiting … for something … I got nothing else left to do, but wait —
LILLY. Franky —
FRANKY. I don't even know anymore what I'm waiting for. And Tony is just so — God, I shouldn't be talking to you about this.
LILLY. Why not?
FRANKY. There's just a lot about your cousin you don't know and it's not really my place to tell you. *(Pause. Lilly looks at Franky.)*
LILLY. I really doubt there is anything about Tony I don't know.
FRANKY. Then you know he cheats.
LILLY. Yes.
FRANKY. Shit —
LILLY. He hasn't told me, if that's what you're thinking. He likes to think I only see him in a certain way. Though, he forgets I know him in every way. Besides, Tony likes to keep secrets. It makes him feel important. Do you know who she is?
FRANKY. It's a small town.

LILLY. It is.
FRANKY. It's fucken humiliating.
LILLY. Who is she?
FRANKY. Tanya Graves.
LILLY. *(Laughing.)* You can't be serious.
FRANKY. It's not funny, Lilly.
LILLY. You can't take that seriously, Franky. She's fucked every guy in town. She makes my mother look like a saint.
FRANKY. Don't talk that way about your mother.
LILLY. Sorry.
FRANKY. You should be. You only have one mother, you know?
LILLY. I know, Franky. Look, even if it did mean — look, she's nothing, Tony would never, Tony loves you —
FRANKY. You sound like them.
LILLY. Who?
FRANKY. Everyone. Like it shouldn't matter. Like I should just be happy he comes home to me at night —
LILLY. He really loves you, Franky. He loves me and he loves you —
FRANKY. Well, maybe I don't want to be loved like that. Maybe I want to be the first and only. I thought you of all people wouldn't give me the same old bullshit line. I thought you'd talk different to me. I thought 'cause you always wanted more, but you just want me to stay put like everyone else. Stay put and be quiet. Why would you ask that of me, Lilly? You never seem to ask it of yourself.
LILLY. That's not what I meant —
FRANKY. Isn't it?
LILLY. I just meant —
FRANKY. I know, I know, Lilly — *(She turns to go inside.)*
LILLY. *(Grabbing her arm.)* Franky, I swear I didn't —
FRANKY. What did you mean, then?
TONY. *(Offstage.)* Franky! Hey Franky, I see you up there. *(Lilly drops Franky's arm. Tony, Drew and Vin enter onto the porch. Tony is holding up a bottle of 151 rum. He does a rebel yell.)* We're gonna party tonight!
FRANKY. *(To Tony.)* Why did you buy that? We have a bottle in the house.
TONY. Yeah, but we didn't have one in the car.
FRANKY. How much you boys have in the car then?
DREW. We just had a few shots, Franky.
FRANKY. A few shots. *(She looks at the bottle.)* You drank half the

bottle. *(The boys move inside to the living room, the women follow. Vin crosses into the living room and the others follow him. They all sit. Vin starts to roll a joint.)*
VIN. *(To Lilly.)* Wait till you try this shit.
LILLY. That good?
VIN. Last of the cash crop from Higgin's farm.
TONY. How'd you get that?
VIN. He likes me.
TONY. He doesn't like anybody.
VIN. Well, he likes me. I work hard for him.
DREW. Everybody likes you.
VIN. 'Cause of my sweet personality.
TONY. Nobody thinks you're sweet but your mother.
DREW. Not even his mother thinks he's sweet.
VIN. Come, come. I'm loved by all. *(He lights the joint and hands it to Lilly.)* Now give that a try.
LILLY. Jesus, it's smooth —
VIN. Give it two seconds and it'll hit you like a ton of bricks. I bet none of your friends over in Northampton ever smoked something like this.
DREW. Hey, I know a joke.
VIN. No, Drew —
DREW. It's a fucken good joke —
TONY. You've never told a good joke in your life —
VIN. He only knows three —
DREW. What keeps Northampton from flooding?
VIN. We've heard this one.
DREW. Yeah, but what keeps Northampton from flooding?
VIN. We've heard this one.
DREW. You've heard it 'cause I told it to you. So … what keeps Northampton from flooding?
LILLY. OK, what?
DREW. All the dykes. *(He laughs, so does Tony.)*
TONY. Hey, that's true. Isn't that true Lill?
LILLY. Sure is, it's the lezzie capital of the world.
FRANKY. You ever talk to one?
LILLY. I can't help it. They're all over campus. In fact the girl that runs my dorm is one.
FRANKY. How do you know?
LILLY. Her and her girlfriend kiss all over the place.

FRANKY. No shit?
VIN. Now that would be a sight. Frisky co-eds, women loving women.
DREW. Nothing wrong with that!
VIN. Girl-on-girl action.
TONY. I feel myself getting higher right now.
FRANKY. Real cute, Tony.
LILLY. It's not like that. I mean, I think they're really in love.
VIN. That's not love.
LILLY. It's not?
VIN. No, I got to hand it to you, Lilly, getting an education in a place like that. *(He lights the joint, takes a hit and they begin to pass it around.)*
LILLY. What do you mean?
VIN. I mean you got all the freaks with you over there. People with purple hair and shit, right?
LILLY. And pink and red, the fucken colors of the rainbow.
VIN. I guess they wanna think that makes them different.
LILLY. They just want to express themselves.
VIN. Express themselves for what?
LILLY. They just —
VIN. Well it's nice they got all that time and money. You need time and money to express yourself. The rest of us are just trying to earn a living.
TONY. Lilly's dating a rich guy with a BMW.
LILLY. No I'm not, Tony. I'm not dating anyone.
DREW. How rich?
TONY. Very rich. What's his name again Lilly?
LILLY. His name's Billy but I'm not dating him, Tony, he's just a friend. I've told you that.
TONY. That's right, Billy. He's got a Beemer, 2002. Lilly wants me to meet him.
DREW. Maybe he'll let you drive the car.
TONY. I never like your boyfriends, Lilly.
LILLY. He's not my boyfriend, Tony. I never have boyfriends.
TONY. That's not true. You had that scrawny kid in high school.
LILLY. Who?
TONY. The one with all that hair. The girls all loved him for his blond hair.
LILLY. That was long time ago, Tony.

TONY. A fucken BMW.

VIN. Well good for him. I'll work my whole life and never get a car like that. It's not fair.

LILLY. I know.

VIN. *(To Lilly.)* You know how hard it is? *(To the room.)* We work hard don't we — ?

TONY. We do —

LILLY. I know but he's a good — you'd like him, Vin, you'd all like him. We almost drove up here the other day —

DREW. What, he want to buy some pot?

VIN. Yeah, homegrown — I'll sell him some homegrown —

DREW. Money to spare —

VIN. We'll meet his parents — maybe they want some homegrown too —

LILLY. He's my friend, he's just like —

VIN. Us?

LILLY. I didn't mean that —

VIN. Let me tell you something about people like us. People like you and me, Lilly. We remember where we came from. We remember what's important. It's the state of the world today, man, when a man can't walk down the street without some nigger or Puerto Rican getting in the way, you know what I'm saying, Lilly?

LILLY. *(Getting handed the joint and inhaling deeply.)* I know, Vin.

VIN. I'm a goddamn American. My dad worked all his life doing shit. You understand? Slaving. Breaking his fucken back, you understand? To just put meat on the table. And my ma fucking around the way she did. This shit's gotta end. Fuck that! This is my country! I work hard hauling that goddamn cordwood day in and day out. I got some pride. I ain't no shiftless motherfucker living off welfare. I work for a living. I pay for my goddamn beer. I ain't like some people around here who only drink other people's shit.

DREW. What the fuck is that supposed to mean? I put in three bucks.

VIN. Just stay out of this, Drew!

DREW. Don't tell me what to do! I can talk if I want and you're just talking shit! I put in three bucks —

VIN. I'm talking about pride! I'm talking about my father and his father all the way down the line. I'm talking about red-blooded Americans. When it stood for something. When it meant something to say the Pledge of Allegiance at school. Now who am I praying to? Goddamn Mexicans and chinks! Pretty soon they'll be coming up here and I got my gun!

DREW. Why you talking so crazy, huh? Nobody's coming up here.

FRANKY. *(To Lilly.)* You gonna share?

LILLY. I'm sharing, ain't I? I share with you. *(She takes a hit of the joint.)* Yeah. Yeah, you're right, Vin. You are right, the shit's gotta end. I fucked a black man once.

TONY. What the fuck — ?

VIN. Lilly! For God's sake, don't say things like that. Why you gotta be so ugly, girl? What makes you get so ugly?

LILLY. *(Inhaling deeply on the joint.)* I ain't being ugly, I'm just saying, fucked the same as any man. Stuck it in me and moved it around. Came. Just the same. All I'm saying is a prick's a prick. You know what I mean, Vin? *(Franky snickers. Lilly hands her the joint.)*

TONY. You've got some mouth on you sometimes, girl —

LILLY. *(To Tony.)* I'm sorry Tony, you know I —

VIN. What's so funny, Franky?! What you laughing at?!

TONY. Lilly has strong feelings about this prejudice shit, Vin. I just don't talk about it.

VIN. Come on! Listen … Lilly, why you do that, huh? Why would you ever go against your own kind like that? Is that what people over there in Northampton do? Everybody fucking everybody like bunnies?

LILLY. Sure. Sure. *(To Franky.)* Give it back. *(Franky holds the joint in her hand up to Lilly's mouth and Lilly takes a drag.)*

DREW. *(To Franky.)* You do that for me too? *(Franky does.)* We're having a great time.

VIN. Shit! Hand it over here. And give me a beer too. Enough of this chit-chat. Let's get serious. *(Silence.)*

TONY. So Franky, are you gonna put some music on or what?

FRANKY. Yeah. This one?

LILLY. Nope.

VIN. Put Hendrix on.

LILLY. Nope.

DREW. Zeppelin? *(He sings.)* "Gonna ramble on, on my way, I'm gonna find my girl … "

LILLY. *(Laughing.)* God no.

FRANKY. How 'bout this one?

LILLY. No. *(Leaning over her shoulder.)* Here it is.

DREW. What is it?

LILLY. You'll see. *(Franky presses play. A song like "Roadhouse Blues" by The Doors comes on.*)*

TONY. Yes!

VIN. Good choice.

TONY. This is my song! *(He sings along.)*

LILLY. *(To Tony.)* There you go. You happy now?

TONY. *(To Lilly.)* Just about. *(Vin, Drew and Tony all sing along to the chorus of the song.)*

LILLY. *(To Franky.)* I feel like dancing.

FRANKY. You do?

LILLY. Yeah, I do. *(To Tony.)* Tony, I feel like dancing.

TONY. Uh-oh. You that drunk, Lilly?

LILLY. I am. I am that drunk … it's getting bad. I have to do something to make it stop. Dance with me Tony.

TONY. I'm too drunk to dance. Just dance by yourself. You're safe with me. I know when to tell you to stop. Go ahead, you dance and I'll sing. *(He starts singing again. Lilly gets up and starts dancing around the room. She sees Franky.)*

LILLY. *(To Franky.)* Come dance with me.

FRANKY. Lill …

LILLY. What's the matter, don't you dance either?

FRANKY. Not like you do. *(Lilly pulls her up and twirls her around.)*

LILLY. That doesn't matter, just follow me. *(Lilly pulls Franky into her and begins to dance with her in a somewhat sexual manner.)*

TONY. There you go, Lill. There you go, I bet you feel better now. *(Lilly laughs in answer and pulls Franky closer to her. The dancing becomes more obviously sexual. Vin and Drew exchange a glance.)*

DREW. Hey Frank, you're looking a little dizzy. Maybe you better sit down.

LILLY. *(To Franky.)* You're not dizzy, are you?

DREW. Hey Franky, I think you better sit down.

VIN. *(To Drew.)* Let it go, man.

LILLY. *(To Franky, spinning her around.)* You're drunk.

FRANKY. Yeah, I'm drunk.

LILLY. I'm drunk, Tony's drunk, we're all drunk.

TONY. *(He raises his bottle of 151.)* Yee-hawww! *(Lilly falls back onto a chair, pulling Franky onto her lap. She puts her arms around*

* See Special Note on Songs and Recordings on copyright page.

Franky's waist. Franky giggles.)

FRANKY. *(To Lilly.)* That tickles.

DREW. *(Standing up.)* I'm gonna change the music.

VIN. *(To himself.)* Oh shit.

LILLY. I like the music, leave it on.

DREW. I was thinking of something mellow. Something — late night, like now. *(He crosses to Lilly and Franky. He takes Franky's hand and tries to pull her off of Lilly's lap.)* Come on Frank, help me choose the music.

LILLY. *(Holding onto Franky.)* She's happy where she is. *(She nuzzles Franky's neck.)* Aren't you? Isn't she, Tony?

TONY. She sure is. *(Drew crosses to the stereo and starts looking through tapes.)* Leave the music alone, man.

DREW. We just need a change of atmosphere.

LILLY. We want to listen to what's playing.

DREW. I'm just looking.

TONY. *(To Drew.)* Why you still looking through those tapes?

DREW. Just something to do.

TONY. I'm not so drunk that I'm not gonna notice if you change the music.

DREW. I know that. *(Lilly tickles Franky. Franky giggles.)*

TONY. *(To Drew.)* Are you insulting my cousin's taste in my music?

LILLY. *(Giggling.)* Uh-oh, Tony's getting mad.

DREW. I ain't insulting anyone.

LILLY. You aren't insulting anyone.

DREW. The genius speaks.

TONY. Watch out, man …

DREW. Well, she is a genius, AIN'T she?

TONY. You're in my house.

DREW. I know.

TONY. Lilly's family, and that makes this her house too. So when she tells you something, it's the same as me telling you. Now we're both telling you to get away from the stereo and sit down over there by Vin where you belong. You're starting to ruin my buzz. *(Drew doesn't move for a moment. He stares at Tony, then he starts to move slowly back towards Vin.)* Move a little faster. *(He kicks Drew as he walks by.)*

DREW. *(Stopping.)* Don't do that, Tony.

TONY. Yeah? Why not?

DREW. 'Cause I don't like it. *(Tony gets up off the couch. They face each other. Tony pushes Drew lightly.)*

TONY. You like that?
LILLY. *(Laughing.)* Uh-oh.
FRANKY. *(Getting up off Lilly.)* Leave him alone, Tony.
TONY. Stay out of this, Franky. *(Tony pushes Drew again, harder this time.)*
FRANKY. Don't be an asshole, Tony.
DREW. Don't worry, Franky.
TONY. That's right, don't worry, Franky. *(Tony punches Drew. Drew falls to the floor. Tony goes to hit him again. Franky grabs Tony's arm, trying to stop him. Tony turns and pushes her away. Drew gets up off the floor.)*
FRANKY. Would you stop?!
TONY. Stop what? Stop this. *(He punches Drew again.)*
FRANKY. *(Slapping Tony's back.)* Goddamn it! Not in my house! *(She hits his back again. Tony turns around and slaps her across the face. Franky hits him back. He prepares to backhand her across the face.)*
LILLY. Don't! Tony! *(Drew grabs Tony from behind and turns him around before he can hit Franky and punches him. Franky runs for the bedroom and slams the door behind her. Tony and Drew begin to hit each other. They fall over together, smashing beer bottles on the floor. Vin stands up and grabs both Tony and Drew by the back of the neck.)*
VIN. Enough! *(He pushes both of them down onto the floor, away from each other.)* OK, I'm calling it a night. *(Tony starts to go for Drew again. Vin pushes him down and kicks him hard in the stomach.)* Sorry, man, but you'll thank me in the morning. *(He pulls Drew to his feet.)* It's about that time, Drew, don't you think? *(Vin helps Tony up and sits him on the couch. He then propels Drew through the door and out onto the porch. The living room area and bedroom are both dimly lit.)* Well, well. *(Pause.)* Nice night though.
DREW. Feel like a walk?
VIN. Sure. *(Pause. He sniffs the air.)* You always get involved.
DREW. Yup. I do. *(They exit stage left. As they do, the lights crossfade to living room area. Tony is laying on the couch.)*
LILLY. I hate it when you act like that.
TONY. Bullshit, you love it.
LILLY. Why do you pretend to be so stupid?
TONY. 'Cause it's easy. Give me a kiss.
LILLY. You're forgetting who I am. You should sleep out here tonight.
TONY. *(He's passing out.)* Yeah, sure … *(Lilly crosses to the bedroom door and knocks lightly. She opens the door and closes it behind her as*

lights come up. Franky is sitting on the bed.)

LILLY. You OK?

FRANKY. Fine.

LILLY. Good … Tony passed out on the couch.

FRANKY. Yeah.

LILLY. So … can I sleep in here tonight?

FRANKY. Sure.

LILLY. *(She crosses to the bed and sits down. She reaches for Franky's hand.)* I'm pretty drunk, I'm sorry.

FRANKY. I'm drunk too.

LILLY. No, I'm sorry about Tony.

FRANKY. *(She withdraws her hand.)* Me too.

LILLY. *(She takes her hand again.)* He just likes to show off. I had fun dancing at least, did you?

FRANKY. Yeah …

LILLY. God, I'm drunk. Dancing with you made me feel funny. Did you feel funny?

FRANKY. Funny?

LILLY. Yeah, funny. I wanted to hurt him when he touched you like that. I don't like it when he's like that. Every time I see him it's like he's farther away. He never used to do stuff like that, or did he? I guess he did. I always used to be able to talk to Tony. Didn't I? Like today he came and got me when nobody else would. He knew I wanted to come home. He always knows things about me. Doesn't he?

FRANKY. I guess.

LILLY. Am I boring you?

FRANKY. Lilly, it's just that —

LILLY. I don't mean to bore you.

FRANKY. I can't fix it for you, Lilly.

LILLY. Fix what?

FRANKY. Whatever you got that needs fixing. I can't fix anything, I just go around and around.

LILLY. 'Cause he hit you?

FRANKY. No.

LILLY. Because he makes you lonely?

FRANKY. In a way, I guess. Or maybe, it's 'cause in the end everything's lonely. Lilly, what are you doing?

LILLY. I don't know. *(Lilly kisses her. Franky kisses her back and then pushes her away.)*

FRANKY. Whoa, whoa! Fuck! What the fuck was that?!

LILLY. God, that felt good, didn't it? God that felt so — Shit, I want to — You're so beautiful ... *(Touching her.)*

FRANKY. Lilly, you're really drunk. Why don't we just go to sleep? Come on, Lilly, lay down. *(She gently pushes Lilly down on the bed. Lilly grabs her and pulls her down with her onto the bed. Lilly kisses Franky's neck, lying under her.)* Oh shit. Lilly, whoa, whoa, take it easy. You're drunk, OK? Sometimes when people are drunk, you know, shit like this happens. We're just gonna go to sleep and every thing will be fine in the morning.

LILLY. *(Letting go of her.)* You don't like me.

FRANKY. *(Getting off of her.)* Sure I like you, Lill. I like you a lot. It's just time for bed, that's all.

LILLY. No, you don't like me as much as I like you!

FRANKY. Shit. Lilly, I love you ...

LILLY. You don't, you don't!

FRANKY. *(Patting Lilly's shoulder.)* Hey, come on Lilly, it's time for sleep.

LILLY. *(Sitting up and seeming suddenly sober.)* Please, please I want to so badly. I can't stand how bad I want to. You want to too, don't you? *(Lilly leans toward Franky, taking her face in both hands, she kisses her. Lilly pushes Franky back onto the bed, laying on top of her. Franky's arms come around Lilly as they kiss. Lilly kisses Franky's neck. Franky suddenly pushes Lilly off of her. She jumps off the bed and back towards the door. The women stare at each other. Franky reaches the bedroom door.)*

FRANKY. I'm going out to sleep with Tony. You can have the bed.

LILLY. Great, thanks.

FRANKY. Well OK, sleep well. *(She hesitates by the door, looking at Lilly.)*

LILLY. Please don't go.

FRANKY. I ... Jesus, Lilly, Jesus! I don't know. I gotta get out of here. *(Franky opens the bedroom door and stands in the door way. She looks out at Tony on the couch and then back to Lilly. The women look at each other. There is a pause. Franky walks back into the bedroom, closing the door behind her. Lilly looks away.)* Lilly.

LILLY. What?

FRANKY. Look at me.

LILLY. Why?

FRANKY. Because I asked you to. *(Lilly looks at Franky.)* You're a good-looking kid, Lilly.

LILLY. Yeah? What's the operative word there, good-looking or kid?

FRANKY. Good-looking is two words, isn't it? So is this what you've been doing at college?
LILLY. What?
FRANKY. You been kissing all the girls?
LILLY. No.
FRANKY. No? You sure?
LILLY. Yes, I'm fucken sure! What the hell are you still doing in here? Go out to Tony!
FRANKY. Keep your voice down.
LILLY. No!
FRANKY. You asked me not to leave and I didn't. Now I'm asking you to keep your voice down. Do you think you can do that?
LILLY. Yes.
FRANKY. Good. So am I the first girl you ever kissed? Answer me, am I the first?
LILLY. Yes.
FRANKY. Good. I always wanted to be the first at something.
LILLY. What the fuck does that mean? *(Franky crosses to her and pushes her down on the bed and starts kissing her. Pulling away:)* OK, OK.
FRANKY. No, come back, don't stop.
LILLY. Franky, I can't.
FRANKY. Sure you can. You just were.
LILLY. I'm scared.
FRANKY. You're scared? What are you scared of?
LILLY. You.
FRANKY. Me? Nobody's ever been afraid of me in my whole life. What do you got to be afraid of?
LILLY. What you're doing to me.
FRANKY. Yeah? What about what you're doing to me? Maybe you're scared of that? What you gonna do to me, Lilly? *(She touches Lilly.)*
LILLY. *(Pulling away.)* Don't.
FRANKY. Oh come on. What did you think? You think no one was ever gonna say yes to you? Well, I'm saying it. I'm the one that said it. You wanna know? I'm the one who's gonna show you. 'Cause I'm the one who likes the way you feel. *(She pushes Lilly back down on the bed and begins to make love to her. Lights fade down.)*

End of Act One

ACT TWO

Scene 1

A few days later, late afternoon. Vin, Drew and Tony sit on the porch drinking and smoking cigarettes.

TONY. You hear that?
DREW. Yup.
VIN. It's gotta be the granddaddy of all the crickets.
TONY. Rambo cricket.
DREW. Well, Old Man Winter should be claiming him any second now.
TONY. Yup. Drew, what the fuck do you see up there?
DREW. The cosmos, man.
TONY. You hear that, Vin? Our man here is looking at the cosmos.
VIN. Well, somebody's gotta do it, right?
TONY. Yeah.
DREW. You going hunting this year, Tony?
TONY. Yeah. Me and my cousin Herbie.
VIN. Yeah, I can taste venison stew right now.
TONY. *(To Drew.)* You going alone again?
DREW. Yeah.
VIN. The solitary hunter.
DREW. Me, the woods and the deer. Who'll be smarter this year?
VIN. You always bag one.
DREW. I only go for one.
VIN. Yeah, like I said, you always bag one.
TONY. The tourists ought to be coming around pretty soon. Goddamn, those boys will shoot at anything. Remember last year Harper Miller got his foot shot off.
VIN. Harper Miller's a dickweed.
DREW. That kid don't know how to hunt.

TONY. True. Last year he shot four and didn't even eat one.
VIN. No respect.
DREW. Right. Smells good, don't it?
TONY. Yup. Nothing like a fall evening.
VIN. 'Cept a spring evening.
TONY. Different tastes.
VIN. Yup.
DREW. Summer's nice too.
VIN. Left out winter.
TONY. Cold as hell.
DREW. Right.
VIN. Sally's been looking good lately.
TONY. Howards?
VIN. Yup.
TONY. Sally's a good kid.
VIN. Took her to the movies in Westfield the other night.
TONY. No shit? You serious?
VIN. Don't know.
TONY. She serious?
VIN. Don't know that either.
TONY. How 'bout you, Drew?
DREW. Karen LaFountain.
TONY. Damn, Drew! She's one fine girlie.
DREW. Yeah. She's OK. *(A light change, lights come up full on the living room and go dim on the boys. Franky and Lilly are huddled together.)*
FRANKY. *(Touching Lilly's face.)* I always thought you were beautiful.
LILLY. You did?
FRANKY. Yes.
LILLY. Really?
FRANKY. Really. There has always been something about you I wanted to touch. Something inside of you. I've never known how to get to you.
LILLY. Have you gotten to me now?
FRANKY. I think maybe. *(She kisses her.)*
LILLY. Do you like getting to me?
FRANKY. Yes.
LILLY. Have I gotten to you?
FRANKY. Yes Lilly, you have.
LILLY. Good. *(She kisses her.)* You wanna know a secret?

FRANKY. Yes.
LILLY. I've thought about kissing you for a long time.
FRANKY. How long?
LILLY. Since I was fifteen.
FRANKY. Jesus. *(She laughs.)* You should have tried earlier.
LILLY. Let's go in the bedroom.
FRANKY. We can't. They're right outside, they'll hear us.
LILLY. We'll be quiet.
FRANKY. You don't know how to be quiet.
LILLY. We'll be quick. *(She kisses Franky.)*
FRANKY. You're crazy.
LILLY. Please, I can't stand it —
FRANKY. You're such a kid. How old are you?
LILLY. You know how old I am.
FRANKY. Tell me again.
LILLY. Nineteen.
FRANKY. A fucken baby.
LILLY. Spoken from the ripe age of twenty-three.
FRANKY. Yes. Tell me another secret.
LILLY. What kind of secret?
FRANKY. Any kind as long as it's something you've never told anyone else before.
LILLY. OK but then maybe we could go into the bedroom? Or in the car? We could go for a ride in the car and pick up beer?
FRANKY. Maybe, let's see how good the secret is first.
LILLY. My biggest secret?
FRANKY. Yes.
LILLY. I love Tony more than I love my mother.
FRANKY. *(Pulling away from her.)* Wow.
LILLY. What?
FRANKY. Why did you say that?
LILLY. Because it's my biggest secret.
FRANKY. Lilly.
LILLY. Did I do something wrong?
FRANKY. No, it's just that —
LILLY. What? I didn't mean to mess things up — I'm sorry, I — *(Tony, Drew and Vin enter from the porch. Franky hears them and quickly pulls away from Lilly. Lilly reaches for Franky and Franky firmly pushes her hand away.)*
TONY. *(Holding up his beer bottle to show the women.)* We're run-

ning on empty. *(Tony goes to the refrigerator and hand beers to Vin and Drew. He takes one for himself and they all file into the living room area.)* What you two ladies been up to?
FRANKY. Just talking.
TONY. Talking huh? You miss me?
FRANKY. Don't I always? *(Tony sits on the couch between Franky and Lilly. He puts one of his arms around each of them.)*
TONY. My two girls.
LILLY. You don't know the half of it.
DREW. Half of what?
TONY. Lilly's just bullshitting around, Drew, you'll get used to it. She liked seeming wishy-washy.
LILLY. Ambiguous.
TONY. What?
LILLY. The word you want is ambiguous. I like being ambiguous.
TONY. Whatever you say, Lill. *(He leans towards Franky.)* Hey.
FRANKY. Hey. *(Tony kisses Franky. She snuggles up beside him. Tony takes his arm off of Lilly and hugs Franky.)*
LILLY. Must be love.
VIN. Yup.
LILLY. What do you think, Drew? Is it love?
DREW. I'd say so.
LILLY. You would. *(Franky gets up and walks towards the fridge.)*
FRANKY. You want a beer, Lill?
LILLY. No.
FRANKY. Sure?
LILLY. Yes.
FRANKY. I'm right here, I can get one for you.
LILLY. I said no!
VIN. Damn girl, temper, temper. Grab her a beer, Franky. She needs to relax. *(Franky gets a beer for herself and Lilly. She walks back to the couch. She holds the beer out to Lilly. Lilly won't take it. Franky sets the beer on the table and sits back down next to Tony. Silence.)*
LILLY. Well boys, it's time to light one up. Vin, would you do the honors?
VIN. Anything to please a lady. *(He takes out pot, starts to roll.)*
LILLY. That's what I like about you, Vin. You're a real romantic. *(She picks up the beer Franky put in front of her and raises it in toast.)* Here's to romance. Franky, Tony, one of this world's true examples. Faithful, honest and kind, two of my favorite people, here's to you.

(She downs the beer and slams the can down on the table.)

FRANKY. That's your girl! You taught her that.

LILLY. *(To the room.)* Yeah. He's taught me everything I know. *(To Franky.)* But I've learned most of his tricks second-hand. Right Frank? *(Vin hands her the rolled joint.)* Nice job, Vin. *(She raises the joint.)* And here's to marriage, marriage and kids. It's just a matter of time. It's inevitable for a girl like you, Franky. How many you gonna have?

TONY. Four.

LILLY. Four? Wow, you're gonna be really busy. That's just what we need, a whole new flock of Marinos, right, Tony? Whattaya think? You think you'll name one after me? *(She lights the joint, inhales and holds it out to Franky.)* You gonna name one after me, Franky? You gonna create a whole new Lilly?

FRANKY. *(Stands.)* I have to go to work.

LILLY. Yeah? *(She hands the joint to Tony.)* I guess it's just me and the boys tonight. No girls night out this evening, right Frank? I guess tonight we have more of a boy thing going on.

FRANKY. *(Kisses Tony.)* Bye baby. *(She starts to leave.)*

LILLY. Kiss your future cousin-in-law goodbye, baby. We have a whole lifetime of this shit to look forward to. *(Pause. Franky looks at her.)* Well?

FRANKY. You all have a good night without me. *(She exits.)*

LILLY. Whelp … let's go boys. Let's get fucked up. *(She holds her hand out to Vin who now has the joint. Vin looks over to Tony who shakes his head no.)*

TONY. You're fucked up already, aren't you, Lill?

LILLY. I guess. *(She holds out her hand for the joint again. Vin puts the joint out.)*

TONY. You're acting kinda crazy, aren't you?

LILLY. Yeah.

TONY. You need to settle down, don't you?

LILLY. I guess.

TONY. Yeah, I guess you do. Well, tonight's a good night for some pool.

VIN. I could do with some pool. Drew?

DREW. I can always do with some pool.

TONY. Why don't you guys wait for me on the porch while I say good night to my cousin. *(Vin and Drew stand up. Vin ruffles Lilly's hair. He motions to the joint he put out in the ashtray.)*

DREW. See you, Lilly.

VIN. I left you a little present kid, enjoy yourself. *(They exit out onto the porch. Lighting a cigarette, he sings:)* "I feel a bad moon a rising, I feel trouble on the way — "

DREW. Give me a cigarette.

VIN. *(Handing him one.)* When you gonna get a job, man? I'm tired of supporting your ass.

DREW. Fuck you.

VIN. Touchy, touchy.

DREW. You think it's funny.

VIN. I didn't say that.

DREW. There's some shit going on here, that's all I'm saying.

VIN. So? There's shit going on everywhere, why should here be any different. Haven't you learned yet, if you leave things alone they go away. *(Lilly and Tony in the living room.)*

TONY. What the fuck is wrong with you?

LILLY. I don't know.

TONY. You gotta make scenes like that?

LILLY. No.

TONY. You get hot-blooded just like your mother.

LILLY. Don't say that.

TONY. You make me look like shit in front of my friends.

LILLY. I'm sorry.

TONY. You shouldn't talk to Franky like that.

LILLY. I know.

TONY. She doesn't deserve it.

LILLY. I know.

TONY. I'm gonna let you keep the rest of that joint 'cause I love ya and you're on vacation. But I don't want to see you like this again. It's not attractive on you. You hear me?

LILLY. Yeah.

TONY. You hear me?

LILLY. I hear you, Tony. *(Tony enters onto the porch.)*

TONY. Pool?

VIN. And brewsky. *(They all exit.)*

Scene 2

Three A.M. the next morning. Tony is asleep in the bedroom. Lilly sits in the living room reading. Franky returns from waitressing.

FRANKY. Hey.
LILLY. Hey. *(She continues to read. Pause.)*
FRANKY. It's fucking freezing out and the goddamn defrost doesn't work.
LILLY. Tony's asleep in the bedroom.
FRANKY. OK … is there any beer left or did you guys drink it all?
LILLY. *(Looking up.)* Do I look drunk to you?
FRANKY. No.
LILLY. Well then, I guess there's beer in the fridge. *(Franky goes to the fridge and gets out a beer.)* There's half a joint too, if you want it, Vin left it for me when the boys went out.
FRANKY. They went out?
LILLY. Yeah, to play pool.
FRANKY. You weren't invited?
LILLY. Nope. *(She goes back to reading. Franky stands waiting. Lilly ignores her.)*
FRANKY. So, I'm waiting.
LILLY. Waiting for what?
FRANKY. Waiting for a fucken apology!
LILLY. Keep your voice down, you'll wake up Tony.
FRANKY. Now you care about Tony?
LILLY. Yeah, he needs his sleep. He's got to work in the morning.
FRANKY. Fuck you.
LILLY. Shit …
FRANKY. Shit, huh? Shit … that scene you pulled earlier. Jesus fucken Christ, you're just lucky I didn't slap you across the face right in front of them.
LILLY. You never would. You're too scared.
FRANKY. Scared? Of course I'm scared. You should be too. Don't you get it? That's Tony in there. Your Tony, my Tony.

LILLY. So?

FRANKY. So? Don't pretend to be stupid. Do you want to hurt him?

LILLY. No.

FRANKY. Do you want to hurt me?

LILLY. No.

FRANKY. You could have fooled me. You were downright ugly.

LILLY. Well, I'm sorry then.

FRANKY. You don't sound sorry. *(She turns to go.)*

LILLY. You leaving now?

FRANKY. I'm going to bed.

LILLY. Before you apologize.

FRANKY. Excuse me?

LILLY. Well, you got your "I'm sorry." Now I want mine.

FRANKY. Really, fuck you, Lilly.

LILLY. That's not a very inventive comeback Franky. You've used it twice now. Next time try to come up with something better. *(She goes back to reading her book.)*

FRANKY. *(Crossing to her and pulling the book out of her hand.)* Don't you dare play that game with me. I won't have it.

LILLY. What? You think just 'cause you fuck me, you get to be as smart as me?

FRANKY. I'm gonna slap you.

LILLY. Say you're sorry!

FRANKY. Jesus, for what?

LILLY. You didn't stand by me.

FRANKY. What?

LILLY. You could have stood by me. You didn't have to pretend I didn't exist. That we didn't exist. You didn't have to act like, like you hadn't just kissed me, like, like —

FRANKY. They'd just walked in. I was protecting us. I was protecting Tony. I mean, we both want to protect Tony —

LILLY. You were protecting yourself.

FRANKY. Yeah? So what? You sure as hell can't do it. And neither can Tony. Goddamn right I was protecting myself, because somebody here has to do it. If I'm protected, we're all protected.

LILLY. I'm not just for fun.

FRANKY. What?

LILLY. I'm real, Franky.

FRANKY. What?

LILLY. I'm something real. You know that.

FRANKY. What are you talking about now?
LILLY. You know what I'm talking about and you know what I mean.
FRANKY. That doesn't change what you did.
LILLY. And it doesn't change what you did either.
FRANKY. Fine. I'm going to bed.
LILLY. Good, go to bed. Tony's waiting for you.
FRANKY. You're unbelievable. *(She exits into the bedroom.)*

Scene 3

The next day. Lilly sits in the living room reading. Drew enters from the porch.

DREW. Hey.
LILLY. Hey. How was pool?
DREW. Like pool always is. You win a little, you lose a little.
LILLY. I lose a lot.
DREW. It just takes practice. If you practiced —
LILLY. I don't have time to practice.
DREW. That's right. What are you reading?
LILLY. Just school work.
DREW. You're on vacation.
LILLY. Doesn't mean there isn't reading over the break.
DREW. For a test?
LILLY. A paper. *(Drew crosses to Lilly and takes the book from her.)*
DREW. *(Looking at the book.) The Essential Works of Marxism*?
LILLY. Not all of them. Just "The Communist Manifesto."
DREW. Why would you read that?
LILLY. 'Cause it's required reading.
DREW. That's weird.
LILLY. Why?
DREW. 'Cause why would you study something you know is wrong?
LILLY. I wouldn't say it's wrong —
DREW. Communism is un-American.
LILLY. Well that's certainly true, up to a point. Communism is

not capitalism. *(She laughs.)*
DREW. Why are you laughing?
LILLY. No reason.
DREW. You laughing at me?
LILLY. No, Drew.
DREW. Yes, you were.
LILLY. I wasn't.
DREW. Yeah, you were laughing with yourself. 'Cause you didn't think I could understand the joke. Little joke, in your own head. I could understand it if you explained it to me. I could understand it, if I read it probably.
LILLY. Of course you could.
DREW. Don't talk to me like that.
LILLY. Like what?
DREW. Like you're talking to a child.
LILLY. I didn't mean —
DREW. Then what did you mean? *(He hands the book back to Lilly.)*
LILLY. *(Catching Drew's hand.)* Hey, *(Holding Drew's hand and holding the book up with the other.)* it's just a book.
DREW. I know it's a book.
LILLY. Don't be afraid of it.
DREW. I'm not afraid of it.
LILLY. *(Dropping Drew's hand.)* Sure you are. You're terrified of it. You and everybody in this house. Afraid of words on a page.
DREW. Maybe, I'm not afraid of it. Maybe I just don't like it.
LILLY. Maybe.
DREW. Maybe, I just don't care.
LILLY. Yeah, maybe.
DREW. And that's allowed, you know Lilly? It's allowed for me not to care. 'Cause I don't. I don't care.
LILLY. I don't believe you. *(They look at each other. A beat.)*
DREW. Is Franky around?
LILLY. I haven't seen her.
DREW. Tell her I stopped by. *(He exits out onto the porch. The lights follow him, up on the porch, down on Lilly. Drew lights a cigarette as Franky enters and crosses up onto the porch. She is holding a grocery bag.)*
FRANKY. Hey, Drew.
DREW. Hi.
FRANKY. Tony's workin'.
DREW. I was looking for you.

FRANKY. Yeah? You want a beer or something?
DREW. No.
FRANKY. What's up?
DREW. Same old thing.
FRANKY. Just want to bullshit?
DREW. What you got in the bag?
FRANKY. Groceries. I was gonna make some breakfast for Lilly. You want some?
DREW. Breakfast, huh? Naw … Nice day out. I've been wandering. I took a walk up Suicide Hill.
FRANKY. You call that a walk? That's not a hill, it's more like a mountain.
DREW. I hung around up there for a while. You know at night you can see as far as Holyoke, sometimes Springfield. I stayed up there. Then I came down.
FRANKY. You just coming from there then?
DREW. Naw. I stopped at Charlie's for a few. Played some pool and shit. You know. Then I took a little walk down Upper Russell Road. I walked for a while. I got as far as my father's church. You know the one.
FRANKY. Sure.
DREW. I did a lot of walking. It's good to walk sometimes, don't you think? I mean distance can be a mental thing. You just decide something and then there you are. If a decision is strong enough, it can take you anywhere. That's the problem with decisions. Y'know you can make them casually, like getting dressed in the morning, forget you made them and then blam, there they are, staring you in the face. I got pretty angry today, looking at that church, Frank. I thought about burning it down. I'd start the fire early Sunday morning. So when they all pulled up, y'know, to get their weekly taste of God, the church would be burning, almost all burned up. What do ya think they'd do then? It would be pretty funny to see the look on their faces, don't you think? Where would they go to believe? They'd have nowhere to go, except their homes. People never believe in their own homes. They get all dressed up for God, do their hair and shit. Not in their homes though, they're too busy trying to fuck somebody else's wife or girlfriend. You know, Frank, people around here, they're just bored and bored people ain't nice people, Frank.
FRANKY. Some people try to believe, Drew. I think maybe we're

those kind of people. And sure sometimes the things we try to believe in don't seem to make sense. But I guess that's part of believing, trying to believe they do.

DREW. Yeah, maybe. And sometimes the things we try to believe in lead us further into believing in nothing at all. Sometimes the prettiest things in the world are flat out poison.

FRANKY. Well there's only one way to find out which is which and that's carrying it through. And sometimes that can be fun. The best fun you ever had.

DREW. Yeah, I know how it goes. *(Pause.)* I just felt like talking, you know. I think I'm gonna head over to Charlie's, 'nough said for now.

FRANKY. Well OK, thanks for stopping by … It's always good to see you Drew, to talk, you know that.

DREW. Yeah, yeah I know. You be good now, you hear? *(He exits. Franky watches him go. Lilly enters onto the porch.)*

LILLY. Hi.

FRANKY. Hi. Did you sleep well?

LILLY. Not really. You?

FRANKY. No. I got us stuff for breakfast.

LILLY. Oh …

FRANKY. Yeah, I got eggs, eggs and bacon.

LILLY. That's nice.

FRANKY. Yeah, so let's go inside.

LILLY. I need some air.

FRANKY. Oh …

LILLY. I thought I'd go for a walk. Maybe say hi to my Mom.

FRANKY. OK, but can we have breakfast first?

LILLY. I need to get out of here for a while, Franky. I really need …

FRANKY. OK, OK sure, I'll just wait for you to get back.

LILLY. Don't, I mean, don't wait, I just, I just need to …

FRANKY. OK. It's OK. *(She touches Lilly.)* I'll be here when you get back.

LILLY. OK, OK that's, that's good.

FRANKY. Good. *(Lilly exits offstage. Franky turns and enters the house.)*

Scene 4

The lights are up in the bedroom. Franky and Tony sit on the bed. Lilly enters through the porch door into the living room area and sits on the couch. She can hear everything in the next room.

FRANKY. Did you hear that? Was that her?
TONY. I didn't hear anything. God, you're jumpy.
FRANKY. Where do you think she went? You think she went to Charlie's?
TONY. She knows she's not allowed at Charlie's.
FRANKY. She's a teenager, Tony. Did you listen when you were a teenager?
TONY. Hell, I don't listen now.
FRANKY. Very cute.
TONY. You need to relax about it.
FRANKY. I'm worried about her coming home. Where do you think she went? Over to Charlie's, right? You think she's gonna bring some guy back here? I don't want that shit going on in my house. You hear me, Tony? This isn't some place for her to come and fuck some guy I have to deal with on my way to work in the morning. She wouldn't do that, would she, Tony? I mean she wouldn't bring some guy back here?
TONY. She's not that type of girl.
FRANKY. What type is that?
TONY. You know, she's like you.
FRANKY. Whatta you mean by that?
TONY. She's the girl you marry.
FRANKY. Not the girl you fuck.
TONY. Don't talk like that.
FRANKY. Why not? Don't you like to hear me swear? My mouth's good enough for your —
TONY. Jesus Christ, settle down. What's wrong?
FRANKY. Nothing.
TONY. Is this about last night?
FRANKY. Whattaya mean?

TONY. You shouldn't take it personally, she gets a little excited sometimes. She's had too much to drink.
FRANKY. No, she hadn't. She was just —
TONY. I talked to her.
FRANKY. When?
TONY. Last night.
FRANKY. About what?
TONY. I told her not to treat you that way. You're the woman of this house.
FRANKY. Jesus, Tony.
TONY. What? You are the woman of this house, aren't you? Of our house?
FRANKY. I guess.
TONY. What does that mean?
FRANKY. You know what that means.
TONY. I've loved you for a long time, Franky. You know that.
FRANKY. Yes, and I've loved you.
TONY. I loved you in high school.
FRANKY. I didn't know that.
TONY. I was a boy.
FRANKY. You had lots of girlfriends.
TONY. I'm a man now.
FRANKY. And you still have lots of girlfriends.
TONY. Do you just want to pick a fight with me?
FRANKY. I don't know. Maybe.
TONY. I want to have children with you.
FRANKY. Oh Tony …
TONY. What? I'd be a good dad. Look at how well Lilly's turned out.
FRANKY. It's different when you're married.
TONY. We're basically married now.
FRANKY. When you're married you forsake all others. Things would have to be different.
TONY. What are you talking about? I just said I want you to marry you.
FRANKY. No actually, you never said marry. I did. *(Pause.)*
TONY. I'm not always good. But I'm a good man. You know that. Besides, what's one thing got to do with the other?
FRANKY. A wife is different than a girlfriend. A wife must be honored.
TONY. I honor you, Franky.

FRANKY. Yes. But not enough.

TONY. I'd never leave you, baby. You know that. No matter what I do, I'll come home to you. I've been looking at Lilly —

FRANKY. What does Lilly have to do with this?

TONY. Nothing except she's going back to school in a couple days, you know?

FRANKY. So, don't you think I know that?

TONY. Franky, look, I'm only saying Lilly's always thinking about her future, working for it, you know? Having her around always reminds me of that. And I want to work for mine, too. And I want my future to be with you and only you. You are the thing I need most in the world. Franky? … Franky, please? I'm not that bad, am I? *(Franky goes to him.)* You could do with me, couldn't you?

FRANKY. I could do with you, Tony.

TONY. Franky will you marry me? *(Franky kisses him and pulls him down onto the bed with her. She lays on top of him. Lights down on them and lights down on Lilly listening.)*

Scene 5

Later the same night. Tony and Franky are asleep in the bedroom. Lilly enters and stands at the bottom of the bed watching them. She reaches out and touches Franky's foot lightly. She then moves around to the side of the bed and shakes Tony's shoulder.

LILLY. Tony, wake up. Tony? *(Tony rolls over and looks at her.)* Wanna play catch? *(Lilly picks up a glove from off the floor and shows it to him.)*

TONY. What time is it?

LILLY. Three A.M.

TONY. We won't be able to see the ball, Lill. Why don't we play tomorrow? *(He lays back down and turns away from her.)*

LILLY. We'll be able to see, there's a street lamp.

TONY. Do you need to talk, Lilly?

LILLY. Please, I need you. *(Tony gets up and gets dressed. Lilly picks up the ball and gloves. They walk out, through the kitchen area, out onto the porch and from the porch onto the bare stage in front of the set. There is a circle of light center stage. They stand on opposite sides of the circle of light at its edges. Lilly tosses Tony a glove. He catches it and puts it on. They toss the ball back and forth in silence for a moment. Tony waits for Lilly to begin. After a moment Tony catches the ball, walks over to Lilly, puts down his gloves and hugs her.)*

TONY. What's wrong Lilly?

LILLY. Everything.

TONY. Now come on, not everything can be wrong, can it?

LILLY. You know my secrets, don't you, Tony?

TONY. I think so —

LILLY. 'Cause every morning you'd drive me to school, 'cause of how the kids treated me on the bus, you know how they'd —

TONY. That was a long-time ago. You're somewhere else now. You're somewhere safe —

LILLY. I'm safe 'cause of you, right? 'Cause you drove me to school and to my college interview and came by on Saturday nights to protect me from my mom and the guys she brought home from the bar —

TONY. Lilly, it's OK. I love you. *(Pause.)*

LILLY. I made a mistake.

TONY. So?

LILLY. I made a bad mistake.

TONY. OK.

LILLY. It's not OK!

TONY. Settle down —

LILLY. Tony ... I wasn't looking and I kinda, it's like I fell down.

TONY. That's OK. You get up again. One thing you can say about Marinos, we're fighters. That's one good thing you can say about us.

LILLY. I'm so tired. I've never been this tired before, Tony. There's all these things I try not to do. I mean, I've been a pretty good girl, don't you think?

TONY. Sure.

LILLY. I always do all my homework and write all my papers and I show up, Tony, honestly I do.

TONY. I know, Lill.

LILLY. No matter what happens I always seem to be able ... but there is some things I've never told you, things I wanted to do, things I wanted to try, to feel ... you know?

TONY. Sure, Lill.

LILLY. It's like smoke keeps coming into me. I don't wanna get up, you know? Everything keeps moving so fast in these bright colors. Just when I think I've got the color, it's not blue, it's red. I don't understand, that's the truth, Tony.

TONY. Well, you got to get up.

LILLY. You never get up and you're OK. It's not like you're dead. You're breathing and eating and fucking, right? Right?!

TONY. I get up in my own way.

LILLY. Oh, bullshit. You stopped getting up years ago. Why do I always have to be the one to get up? Lilly this and Lilly that. Maybe I'm not any of those things. Have you thought of that? Maybe I'm just an idea in your head. And maybe that idea is all you have. I mean, what do you really got, Tony?

TONY. I've got a car and I have Franky, and for me that's something. I'm not you, Lilly, I never said I was.

LILLY. Yeah, you have Franky, you have Franky. You know what? You treat her like shit. Tell me about Tanya.

TONY. What's this about, Lilly?

LILLY. Franky told me. She told me about you and Tanya.

TONY. So?

LILLY. So. That's all you have to say?

TONY. Well, it's my business. Isn't it?

LILLY. I need you to tell me.

TONY. Why, Lilly? Why does this matter? It's got nothing to do with me and you.

LILLY. I have something to tell you. And if you tell me this first, it's gonna help me. Please help me, Tony.

TONY. Jesus, Lill …

LILLY. What's she like in bed?

TONY. She's a fuck.

LILLY. And what's that like?

TONY. I don't know. We don't talk much. We get drunk, go somewhere and fuck, you know.

LILLY. Do I?

TONY. Sure. How many of the people you've slept with have you cared about?

LILLY. One. What's Franky like?

TONY. What do you mean?

LILLY. What's she like in bed?

TONY. Good. The best I ever had.

LILLY. 'Cause you love her, right?

TONY. Yeah, that, and she's just, y'know? Good.
LILLY. So why do you sleep with Tanya then?
TONY. 'Cause I can. *(Pause.)* A man has to do something to let himself know he's wanted. Everyone has to feel like a star in some way, Lill. You got college. I got Tanya.
LILLY. So you have an answer for everything you do? You know why you do it?
TONY. I guess.
LILLY. *(Pause.)* Remember the closet?
TONY. No Lilly.
LILLY. Why not?
TONY. Because I don't want to.
LILLY. Why not?
TONY. It's better left that way.
LILLY. Why?
TONY. Jesus! *(He goes and sits on the porch steps.)* Is this what you wanted to talk about?
LILLY. We never have.
TONY. What's to say?
LILLY. We didn't see anything wrong with it then.
TONY. We were kids.
LILLY. I liked it with you. *(Pause.)* How come you never tried, y'know, tried…? Why didn't we go all the way?
TONY. Who knows.
LILLY. Do you ever think about it?
TONY. Sometimes.
LILLY. When?
TONY. When I see you.
LILLY. All the time when you see me?
TONY. No. It's a passing thought, that's all, Lill.
LILLY. You were the first boy ever to kiss me.
TONY. Shit.
LILLY. You were the first everything.
TONY. I guess.
LILLY. You taught me to drive.
TONY. Yeah.
LILLY. Smoke a joint.
TONY. Sure.
LILLY. Kiss a girl.
TONY. What?

LILLY. I pretended I was you, did it like I thought you would. Like I always do the first time except you weren't actually there to show me, though in a way you were. And it was the first time, is the first time I wish you weren't, you know, here.
TONY. What the fuck are you talking about, Lilly?
LILLY. I kissed a girl.
TONY. OK.
LILLY. That's it.
TONY. Well, you've always been a little weird, Lill. I mean you don't really fit here, do you? I mean you never have. Don't take it wrong. That's why I love you so much. You fit somewhere else, you know? I guess at that school. I mean I fit here, I like it here. OK. You're still my girl, just maybe you know you shouldn't tell anyone else, they might get the wrong idea. *(Pause.)*
LILLY. I've been having sex with Franky.
TONY. Yeah, right. *(He gets up.)* I'm going back to bed, Lilly.
LILLY. *(Lilly grabs his arm.)* Tony, it's true.
TONY. Don't say any more, Lilly. I'm going back to bed. Do you understand me? Just leave it alone.
LILLY. Tony —
TONY. I mean it. Stop talking —
LILLY. I've never loved anyone before except you and now I —
TONY. Lilly —
LILLY. Tony —
TONY. I've never been good at anything in my whole life. Not anything you could put your hands on. But I've always been good at loving you, haven't I?
LILLY. Tony, I —
TONY. I've been good at loving you. It's the only thing I can point to. I can point to you. I've always known you were special. And I've been good at protecting that special-ness. And you got to ask yourself, if I wasn't so good at it, would you even have any of it left? When you protect something, care for something, make sure it grows, in a way you own a part of it. I've waited all my life for you to be where you are. Someone who loves me is gonna be something. I'm already counting to days to your graduation. Now, I'm going in and you're keeping your mouth shut. *(Turns to go.)*
LILLY. Maybe I could.
TONY. *(With his back to her.)* What?
LILLY. Maybe I could be something without you.

TONY. Don't ever say that again.
LILLY. I'm gonna do it again, Tony. I'm gonna do it as long as Franky lets me. And I have to tell you. Who else can I tell?
TONY. *(Tony turns and grabs Lilly, he begins to shake her.)* Franky's mine, goddamn it! Don't you have enough things of your own? I've got one good thing in my life and you got everything! Why'd you have to go and fuck me up like this? I told you to stop talking, didn't I?! Didn't I?! I'd share anything with you, don't you understand that? I always protect you. I know you're better than me. Don't you think I know that? You had to prove it. You fucken cunt, you whore, don't make me, don't make me —
LILLY. I'm sorry, Tony. Tony, stop! I love you. Please, I'm sorry? *(He continues to shake her. Lilly throws her arms around his neck. She tries to hug him and stop the shaking at the same time. Tony pushes her away from him, holding her by the arms. She tries to move into him to hug him again. As she does, they bump heads and mouths. They end up kissing. Tony lets go of her arms. She puts her arms around him.)* It's OK. Tony. It's OK. I'll give it back. Here, let me give it back. *(Lights down on them kissing.)*

Scene 6

Late afternoon the next day. Lilly is standing on the porch smoking a cigarette. Franky enters stage right in her waitress uniform. She crosses to the porch and up to Lilly.

FRANKY. Hey. There you are —
LILLY. Good, I've been waiting for you, Franky —
FRANKY. Where the hell have you been — ?
LILLY. Because I need to talk to you —
FRANKY. I haven't seen you, I was starting to think —
LILLY. I think I'm losing my mind.
FRANKY. I was thinking about what you said the other night — and you were right in a way — but you know why I don't feel guilty? 'Cause you're the most beautiful thing that's ever happened to me. You've been such a surprise. Such a crazy, beautiful surprise. I don't see why you're so worried. I told you I love you already. It

seems to me that, that should be enough.
LILLY. I heard you with him last night and —
FRANKY. I'm sorry … I didn't know you were home. I never would have, I mean —
LILLY. This situation is very —
FRANKY. I know, but —
LILLY. He loves you —
FRANKY. I know, Lilly, look it's OK —
LILLY. And he's the only thing I ever had, it's just that you, Franky, you, I mean I —
FRANKY. *(Going to touch her.)* Baby, it's OK, all this is just between you and me, and I —
LILLY. I wish it was, Franky, but see I kinda, I kinda lost it —
FRANKY. Do you just want to fight?
LILLY. Are you gonna marry him?
FRANKY. I don't —
LILLY. Do you have any idea of the mess we made — ?
FRANKY. Lilly, things happen, it doesn't mean —
LILLY. It means that every time I come up here for the rest of my life I have to watch you with him and him with you and —
FRANKY. We have a secret together, that's all. A beautiful secret —
LILLY. Bullshit, we have a fucken nightmare —
FRANKY. OK, you want to stop the bullshit, stop pretending you're coming back here. You and I both know that pretty soon this place and me and even Tony are just gonna be a memory. What, in a couple of years, you're still gonna wanna come up here and shoot the shit, drink some beers and —
LILLY. This is my home. I grew up here just like you. Why is everybody always treating me like I'm just passing through?
FRANKY. 'Cause you are.
LILLY. To where? Where the hell do you think I'm going? You think I belong over there — ?
FRANKY. No. But you will. I only fit one place. I fit here. I wish I was you. I wish I could fit anywhere but here.
LILLY. Is that why you fucked me? Is that why you fucken — why you fucken made me think you actually…? Shit! *(She turns and crosses into the living room. Franky follows.)*
FRANKY. Lilly —
LILLY. Don't touch me —
FRANKY. Lilly, hey —

LILLY. I thought, I thought you actually, actually, what have I done — ?

FRANKY. God, you can be so dramatic.

LILLY. Dramatic! I'm nothing but a fuck-up, Franky. Everything I do, I mess up.

FRANKY. *(She crosses to her and pulls her down onto the couch and lays on top of her.)* I thought you were with someone else last night. It made me sick to think of anybody else touching you. *(She kisses her.)* God, you taste so good. *(She kisses her again.)* Oh, you make me feel so good. Every part of you feels good.

LILLY. Franky —

FRANKY. *(Kissing her.)* What's wrong with you, stop talking and be with me.

LILLY. Franky, listen, I told him.

FRANKY. *(Sitting up.)* You did what?

LILLY. I told him. I'm sorry.

FRANKY. Jesus, Lilly.

LILLY. I got confused.

FRANKY. You got confused? Lilly, do you have any idea what you've just done to me —

LILLY. I —

FRANKY. When? When did you tell him?

LILLY. Last night.

FRANKY. *(Laughs.)* 'Cause you heard us and you felt so lonely? And then he forgave you, didn't he? He would forgive you anything.

LILLY. In a way he forgave me, but it won't be the same.

FRANKY. Sure it will. You fuck me and he fucks me and my love is never private and the both of you —

LILLY. It wasn't like that.

FRANKY. No? *(She starts to get up.)*

LILLY. *(Grabbing her hand.)* No I paid him. I paid him, we're even.

FRANKY. What does that mean?

LILLY. Really, I paid him. I paid for both of us and he doesn't blame you. He blames me and, he loves you, he does. And he'll pretend the whole thing never happened, except it did, and him and me we'll never, we'll never be the same. But it won't affect you really, really it won't.

FRANKY. Lilly, what did you do? Lilly —

LILLY. Don't you worry about what I did. I —

FRANKY. Jesus, you're such a kid. Such a little fucken kid. I'm so

mad at you I could kill you.
LILLY. I'm — *(She grabs Franky and kisses her. Franky starts to kiss her back. Tony enters and stands in the kitchen area watching them. He crosses into the living room area. The women hear him and stop. Franky moves away from Lilly. They look at each other.)*
TONY. You two wanna tell me what the fuck you think you're doing? Lilly?
LILLY. Yeah?
TONY. What the fuck are you doing?
FRANKY. Tony —
TONY. Stay the fuck out of this, Franky. Lilly, answer me.
LILLY. I love her, Tony.
TONY. You love her?
LILLY. I …
TONY. You just love everybody, don't you? *(Vin and Drew enter from the porch.)*
DREW. *(Motioning to Vin.)* Look what the cat dragged in.
TONY. Hey, man. Where you been?
VIN. Got some work logging with the Petersons.
TONY. We thought your new girlie was keeping you hostage or something. *(Franky crosses to the couch and sits next to Lilly.)* Hey, Franky, don't I get no kiss?
FRANKY. We got company, Tony.
TONY. So? Come here and give me a kiss. *(Franky squeezes Lilly's knee. She then gets off the couch, crosses to Tony and kisses him on the cheek and then moves away. Tony grabs her by the wrist.)* You call that a kiss?
DREW. Franky, since you're up, you wanna get me another beer? I'm about done with this one.
FRANKY. Sure. *(Franky crosses to the kitchen area. She touches Drew's shoulder as she walks past him.)* Anyone else want one? Lilly?
LILLY. I'm OK Frank, thanks though. *(Franky brings Drew a beer. She has one for herself. She sits back down next to Lilly.)*
DREW. So, how much longer you with us, Lilly?
LILLY. End of the week. It's almost time for me to go home.
DREW. Well, we'll all miss you. You'll have to come back and visit again soon.
TONY. Lilly's anxious to get back, aren't you, Lill? Before you all came in, she was telling me about her new boyfriend. Weren't ya? It's been hard on her. She misses him, right, Lill?
LILLY. Tony …

TONY. What? You don't need to be embarrassed. What was his name again? Anyway, I guess he's a real animal, right, Lill? How many times did he make you come again? See, she tells me everything.
VIN. Shit.
TONY. What was it? Once with his mouth, once with his hand and then finally, the main event. He's a very talented guy, a pro, and this was all in one night, boys.
FRANKY. Don't talk that way to her, Tony.
TONY. Aw come on, Franky, I know you want to know this. He got her talking and everything. *(Mimicking Lilly.)* More! More! Oh baby, yes! YES! That's right, fuck me that way, yes … do it! Do it!
FRANKY. *(Standing up.)* Stop that now!
LILLY. He's just drunk.
TONY. I ain't drunk. She ain't much of a lady, is she boys? For a woman to talk like that, she's gotta be, what we call around here, a whore. Right, Vin?
VIN. I got no opinion on this one, man. *(He starts to get up.)*
TONY. Where are you going?
VIN. I thought I'd head over to Charlie's. I'm in the mood for some pool.
TONY. I need you here, man.
VIN. I think you need to settle down.
TONY. There's been a lot of shit going down around here. Right, Franky?
VIN. Your house, your home, man. This ain't any of my business and I'd like to keep it that way. Drew, you coming?
DREW. Naw, I'm gonna finish my beer.
VIN. Get a fresh one at Charlie's.
DREW. *(Nodding at Franky.)* I'm just gonna finish my beer, man. I'll be right over.
VIN. Suit yourself. *(He exits through the kitchen area, then offstage right.)*
TONY. What's wrong with him?
DREW. Nothing.
FRANKY. Let's go into the bedroom, Tony.
TONY. No.
FRANKY. We can talk in the bedroom.
TONY. Lilly wouldn't like that, would you, Lilly?
LILLY. Drew, why don't we all go down to Charlie's. I think we could all use some air.

TONY. You two aren't going anywhere. *(To Lilly.)* You know you might be smarter than me. But I'm bigger. What would you say if I just punched you in the mouth?
LILLY. Tony …
TONY. Are you starting to cry, Lilly? I don't believe it —
LILLY. Tony, please …
TONY. What are those, crocodile tears?
LILLY. No …
FRANKY. Tony, I wanna go to talk in the bedroom, it's not what you think —
TONY. Not what I think. I bet Lilly knows what I think —
LILLY. No —
TONY. Stop crying —
LILLY. I can't —
TONY. I told you to fucken stop crying, you don't deserve to cry —
FRANKY. Tony, get off her —
TONY. What are you, Lilly? I know what you are. Don't I? I know you inside and out. She don't know you at all — she don't know what a little piece of shit —
FRANKY. *(Moving towards Lilly.)* Give her to me.
TONY. Don't touch her —
FRANKY. Tony —
TONY. I said, don't touch her! *(Drew stands up. Franky freezes. Tony advances on Lilly.)*
FRANKY. Drew…?
TONY. *(To Lilly.)* How many more things are you going to ask of me, Lilly? What else you got up your sleeve?
LILLY. *(Backing away from him.)* Tony, don't —
FRANKY. Drew, I don't want him to hurt her —
TONY. Where you going, Lilly, you weren't running last night —
LILLY. Tony —
TONY. There's nothing of mine I wouldn't have shared with you. Nothing I wouldn't have given you. You know that?
LILLY. Yes.
TONY. But you're turning on me just like I was anyone. And I'm all you really got, Lilly. *(To Franky.)* I think you and Drew better leave. We've got something to settle —
FRANKY. I'm not going anywhere — *(Tony grabs Lilly by the scruff of the neck.)* Tony stop! Let her go! Drew? *(Lilly struggles and hits Tony, freeing herself. Tony recovers and hits Lilly back. She falls to the floor.)*

TONY. You whore!
FRANKY. Don't touch her, don't fucken touch her — *(Franky grabs at Tony. Tony slaps Franky. Drew grabs Tony in a full nelson.)*
DREW. OK Tony, OK. That's enough. *(Tony struggles.)* No, Tony. You're headed somewhere you really don't want to go. That's enough, man. *(Drew drags Tony towards the kitchen area. To Franky:)* I'm taking him to Charlie's. Me and Vin will calm him down.
TONY. *(Struggling.)* I'm gonna kill her, man. I'm gonna kill them both. She can't just come up here and do this shit to me. She can't just come up here and wreck my whole life like this! Can she, Drew? Can she?
DREW. *(Pulling him to the door to the porch.)* I guess she can, man. I guess she can.
TONY. Fuck her! Fuck her completely! Hey, Franky —
FRANKY. No.
TONY. Franky, guess what? Not like you had anything special, you hear me? I had her too, I had her last night! *(Drew pulls Tony out the door onto the porch and offstage left. The women sit in silence. Franky on the couch. Lilly on the floor.)*
LILLY. Franky ...
FRANKY. Jesus, that's what you call paying him?
LILLY. Franky ...
FRANKY. *(Lilly goes to her. Franky pushes her back down.)* Stay down! You stay where you are.
LILLY. OK, OK, but I chose you. I chose you over my own cousin, my best friend.
FRANKY. You had to fuck him first? In my own house?
LILLY. No. I went outside. We were outside.
FRANKY. Jesus, you are one fucked-up family.
LILLY. Come with me. Right now. Come with me. We'll both go. We'll talk in the car. I'll explain everything. I'll make it OK, I'll make things OK. You do have somewhere to go. You can go with me.
FRANKY. You're really crazy, you know that?
LILLY. I'm not leaving you here to have his fucken children. I'm not leaving you here to ... Franky, give me a chance.
FRANKY. It would never work.
LILLY. It could work. It could. You could live with me. Then we wouldn't ever have to come back here and we could get a place and you could take classes too and we could talk about things. And you wouldn't have to stay here and I wouldn't have to be over there

all alone.

FRANKY. Lilly —

LILLY. I know it's bad. I know but I can make it up to you and, please Franky, please, please let me make it up to you —

FRANKY. You're so stupid. How come you had to be so stupid? You're so beautiful and so stupid. I wish, I really wish you could have been different. Here's what's gonna happen. You're going to take the car.

LILLY. You have no courage.

FRANKY. I have more courage than you'll ever know. What, you think I don't love you? What's left for me here? You've taken everything away, haven't you? I'll tell you one thing, I'm not trading him for you. One Marino for another. I'm not gonna go live your life, like it was mine. I'm done with that now. What you see here, this is mine. This is me. I ain't built nothing else. And whether I can or not, that's not your business anymore, is it? You're gonna go. And you're gonna do well. And you might feel like the ugliest motherfucker who ever lived next to all those people. And you might think everything you say and do is wrong. And that's when you're gonna think of me and know it ain't half of what I feel 'cause you already got so far. You already know so much. And you're gonna work, Lilly, and you ain't gonna come back here no more.

LILLY. But I want …

FRANKY. You think everything's about what you want.

LILLY. Please don't make me go.

FRANKY. But Lilly, you want to go. All you've ever wanted to do is go. Don't you remember? Now please, everybody's gone. I'm gonna be alone too. Please give me something I can hold. *(Franky holds the car keys out to Lilly. Lilly hesitates and then takes them.)* I'll send Drew with your stuff. He'll bring my car back.

LILLY. OK … *(Lilly turns to go.)*

FRANKY. Hey.

LILLY. Yeah?

FRANKY. You're gonna do OK.

LILLY. Thanks. I —

FRANKY. I know Lilly, just go home. *(Lilly turns and exits out the front door. Franky listens to the sound of the car starting. She lights a cigarette, sound of car driving away. Franky smokes. Lights down.)*

End of Play

PROPERTY LIST

6-packs of beer
Duffel bag
Clothes
Comb
Cigarettes, lighter
2 baseball gloves, baseball
Bottles of 151 rum
Tapes, albums
Marijuana, rolling paper
Books
Grocery bag
Car keys

SOUND EFFECTS

Car driving by
Car starting, driving away

NEW PLAYS

★ **GUARDIANS by Peter Morris.** In this unflinching look at war, a disgraced American soldier discloses the truth about Abu Ghraib prison, and a clever English journalist reveals how he faked a similar story for the London tabloids. "Compelling, sympathetic and powerful." *–NY Times.* "Sends you into a state of moral turbulence." *–Sunday Times (UK).* "Nothing short of remarkable." *–Village Voice.* [1M, 1W] ISBN: 978-0-8222-2177-7

★ **BLUE DOOR by Tanya Barfield.** Three generations of men (all played by one actor), from slavery through Black Power, challenge Lewis, a tenured professor of mathematics, to embark on a journey combining past and present. "A teasing flare for words." *–Village Voice.* "Unfailingly thought-provoking." *–LA Times.* "The play moves with the speed and logic of a dream." *–Seattle Weekly.* [2M] ISBN: 978-0-8222-2209-5

★ **THE INTELLIGENT DESIGN OF JENNY CHOW by Rolin Jones.** This irreverent "techno-comedy" chronicles one brilliant woman's quest to determine her heritage and face her fears with the help of her astounding creation called Jenny Chow. "Boldly imagined." *–NY Times.* "Fantastical and funny." *–Variety.* "Harvests many laughs and finally a few tears." *–LA Times.* [3M, 3W] ISBN: 978-0-8222-2071-8

★ **SOUVENIR by Stephen Temperley.** Florence Foster Jenkins, a wealthy society eccentric, suffers under the delusion that she is a great coloratura soprano—when in fact the opposite is true. "Hilarious and deeply touching. Incredibly moving and breathtaking." *–NY Daily News.* "A sweet love letter of a play." *–NY Times.* "Wildly funny. Completely charming." *–Star-Ledger.* [1M, 1W] ISBN: 978-0-8222-2157-9

★ **ICE GLEN by Joan Ackermann.** In this touching period comedy, a beautiful poetess dwells in idyllic obscurity on a Berkshire estate with a band of unlikely cohorts. "A beautifully written story of nature and change." *–Talkin' Broadway.* "A lovely play which will leave you with a lot to think about." *–CurtainUp.* "Funny, moving and witty." *–Metroland (Boston).* [4M, 3W] ISBN: 978-0-8222-2175-3

★ **THE LAST DAYS OF JUDAS ISCARIOT by Stephen Adly Guirgis.** Set in a time-bending, darkly comic world between heaven and hell, this play reexamines the plight and fate of the New Testament's most infamous sinner. "An unforced eloquence that finds the poetry in lowdown street talk." *–NY Times.* "A real jaw-dropper." *–Variety.* "An extraordinary play." *–Guardian (UK).* [10M, 5W] ISBN: 978-0-8222-2082-4

NEW PLAYS

★ **THE GREAT AMERICAN TRAILER PARK MUSICAL music and lyrics by David Nehls, book by Betsy Kelso.** Pippi, a stripper on the run, has just moved into Armadillo Acres, wreaking havoc among the tenants of Florida's most exclusive trailer park. "Adultery, strippers, murderous ex-boyfriends, Costco and the Ice Capades. Undeniable fun." *–NY Post.* "Joyful and unashamedly vulgar." *–The New Yorker.* "Sparkles with treasure." *–New York Sun.* [2M, 5W] ISBN: 978-0-8222-2137-1

★ **MATCH by Stephen Belber.** When a young Seattle couple meet a prominent New York choreographer, they are led on a fraught journey that will change their lives forever. "Uproariously funny, deeply moving, enthralling theatre." *–NY Daily News.* "Prolific laughs and ear-to-ear smiles." *–NY Magazine.* [2M, 1W] ISBN: 978-0-8222-2020-6

★ **MR. MARMALADE by Noah Haidle.** Four-year-old Lucy's imaginary friend, Mr. Marmalade, doesn't have much time for her—not to mention he has a cocaine addiction and a penchant for pornography. "Alternately hilarious and heartbreaking." *–The New Yorker.* "A mature and accomplished play." *–LA Times.* "Scathingly observant comedy." *–Miami Herald.* [4M, 2W] ISBN: 978-0-8222-2142-5

★ **MOONLIGHT AND MAGNOLIAS by Ron Hutchinson.** Three men cloister themselves as they work tirelessly to reshape a screenplay that's just not working—*Gone with the Wind.* "Consumers of vintage Hollywood insider stories will eat up Hutchinson's diverting conjecture." *–Variety.* "A lot of fun." *–NY Post.* "A Hollywood dream-factory farce." *–Chicago Sun-Times.* [3M, 1W] ISBN: 978-0-8222-2084-8

★ **THE LEARNED LADIES OF PARK AVENUE by David Grimm, translated and freely adapted from Molière's *Les Femmes Savantes.*** Dicky wants to marry Betty, but her mother's plan is for Betty to wed a most pompous man. "A brave, brainy and barmy revision." *–Hartford Courant.* "A rare but welcome bird in contemporary theatre." *–New Haven Register.* "Roll over Cole Porter." *–Boston Globe.* [5M, 5W] ISBN: 978-0-8222-2135-7

★ **REGRETS ONLY by Paul Rudnick.** A sparkling comedy of Manhattan manners that explores the latest topics in marriage, friendships and squandered riches. "One of the funniest quip-meisters on the planet." *–NY Times.* "Precious moments of hilarity. Devastatingly accurate political and social satire." *–BackStage.* "Great fun." *–CurtainUp.* [3M, 3W] ISBN: 978-0-8222-2223-1

NEW PLAYS

★ **AFTER ASHLEY by Gina Gionfriddo.** A teenager is unwillingly thrust into the national spotlight when a family tragedy becomes talk-show fodder. "A work that virtually any audience would find accessible." *–NY Times.* "Deft characterization and caustic humor." *–NY Sun.* "A smart satirical drama." *–Variety.* [4M, 2W] ISBN: 978-0-8222-2099-2

★ **THE RUBY SUNRISE by Rinne Groff.** Twenty-five years after Ruby struggles to realize her dream of inventing the first television, her daughter faces similar battles of faith as she works to get Ruby's story told on network TV. "Measured and intelligent, optimistic yet clear-eyed." *–NY Magazine.* "Maintains an exciting sense of ingenuity." *–Village Voice.* "Sinuous theatrical flair." *–Broadway.com.* [3M, 4W] ISBN: 978-0-8222-2140-1

★ **MY NAME IS RACHEL CORRIE taken from the writings of Rachel Corrie, edited by Alan Rickman and Katharine Viner.** This solo piece tells the story of Rachel Corrie who was killed in Gaza by an Israeli bulldozer set to demolish a Palestinian home. "Heartbreaking urgency. An invigoratingly detailed portrait of a passionate idealist." *–NY Times.* "Deeply authentically human." *–USA Today.* "A stunning dramatization." *–CurtainUp.* [1W] ISBN: 978-0-8222-2222-4

★ **ALMOST, MAINE by John Cariani.** This charming midwinter night's dream of a play turns romantic clichés on their ear as it chronicles the painfully hilarious amorous adventures (and misadventures) of residents of a remote northern town that doesn't quite exist. "A whimsical approach to the joys and perils of romance." *–NY Times.* "Sweet, poignant and witty." *–NY Daily News.* "Aims for the heart by way of the funny bone." *–Star-Ledger.* [2M, 2W] ISBN: 978-0-8222-2156-2

★ **Mitch Albom's TUESDAYS WITH MORRIE by Jeffrey Hatcher and Mitch Albom, based on the book by Mitch Albom.** The true story of Brandeis University professor Morrie Schwartz and his relationship with his student Mitch Albom. "A touching, life-affirming, deeply emotional drama." *–NY Daily News.* "You'll laugh. You'll cry." *–Variety.* "Moving and powerful." *–NY Post.* [2M] ISBN: 978-0-8222-2188-3

★ **DOG SEES GOD: CONFESSIONS OF A TEENAGE BLOCKHEAD by Bert V. Royal.** An abused pianist and a pyromaniac ex-girlfriend contribute to the teen-angst of America's most hapless kid. "A welcome antidote to the notion that the *Peanuts* gang provides merely American cuteness." *–NY Times.* "Hysterically funny." *–NY Post.* "The *Peanuts* kids have finally come out of their shells." *–Time Out.* [4M, 4W] ISBN: 978-0-8222-2152-4

DRAMATISTS PLAY SERVICE, INC.
440 Park Avenue South, New York, NY 10016 212-683-8960 Fax 212-213-1539
postmaster@dramatists.com www.dramatists.com

NEW PLAYS

★ **RABBIT HOLE by David Lindsay-Abaire.** Winner of the 2007 Pulitzer Prize. Becca and Howie Corbett have everything a couple could want until a life-shattering accident turns their world upside down. "An intensely emotional examination of grief, laced with wit." *–Variety.* "A transcendent and deeply affecting new play." *–Entertainment Weekly.* "Painstakingly beautiful." *–BackStage.* [2M, 3W] ISBN: 978-0-8222-2154-8

★ **DOUBT, A Parable by John Patrick Shanley.** Winner of the 2005 Pulitzer Prize and Tony Award. Sister Aloysius, a Bronx school principal, takes matters into her own hands when she suspects the young Father Flynn of improper relations with one of the male students. "All the elements come invigoratingly together like clockwork." *–Variety.* "Passionate, exquisite, important, engrossing." *–NY Newsday.* [1M, 3W] ISBN: 978-0-8222-2219-4

★ **THE PILLOWMAN by Martin McDonagh.** In an unnamed totalitarian state, an author of horrific children's stories discovers that someone has been making his stories come true. "A blindingly bright black comedy." *–NY Times.* "McDonagh's least forgiving, bravest play." *–Variety.* "Thoroughly startling and genuinely intimidating." *–Chicago Tribune.* [4M, 5 bit parts (2M, 1W, 1 boy, 1 girl)] ISBN: 978-0-8222-2100-5

★ **GREY GARDENS book by Doug Wright, music by Scott Frankel, lyrics by Michael Korie.** The hilarious and heartbreaking story of Big Edie and Little Edie Bouvier Beale, the eccentric aunt and cousin of Jacqueline Kennedy Onassis, once bright names on the social register who became East Hampton's most notorious recluses. "An experience no passionate theatergoer should miss." *–NY Times.* "A unique and unmissable musical." *–Rolling Stone.* [4M, 3W, 2 girls] ISBN: 978-0-8222-2181-4

★ **THE LITTLE DOG LAUGHED by Douglas Carter Beane.** Mitchell Green could make it big as the hot new leading man in Hollywood if Diane, his agent, could just keep him in the closet. "Devastatingly funny." *–NY Times.* "An out-and-out delight." *–NY Daily News.* "Full of wit and wisdom." *–NY Post.* [2M, 2W] ISBN: 978-0-8222-2226-2

★ **SHINING CITY by Conor McPherson.** A guilt-ridden man reaches out to a therapist after seeing the ghost of his recently deceased wife. "Haunting, inspired and glorious." *–NY Times.* "Simply breathtaking and astonishing." *–Time Out.* "A thoughtful, artful, absorbing new drama." *–Star-Ledger.* [3M, 1W] ISBN: 978-0-8222-2187-6